DEAR MRS. MARTIN

&

MOTHER'S DAY

Two One-Act Plays

by Kate Aspengren

SAMUEL FRENCH, INC.

45 WEST 25TH STREET   NEW YORK 10010
7623 SUNSET BOULEVARD HOLLYWOOD 90046
LONDON   TORONTO

**For my parents,
Ed and Mary Lou Aspengren**

Special thanks to Linda Cooper

IMPORTANT BILLING AND CREDIT REQUIREMENTS

All producers of *DEAR MRS. MARTIN and MOTHER'S DAY must* give credit to the Author of the Play in all programs distributed in connection with performances of the Play and in all instances in which the title of the Play appears for purposes of advertising, publicizing or otherwise exploiting the Play and/or a production. The name of the Author *must* also appear on a separate line, on which no other name appears, immediately following the title, and *must* appear in size of type not less than fifty percent the size of the title type.

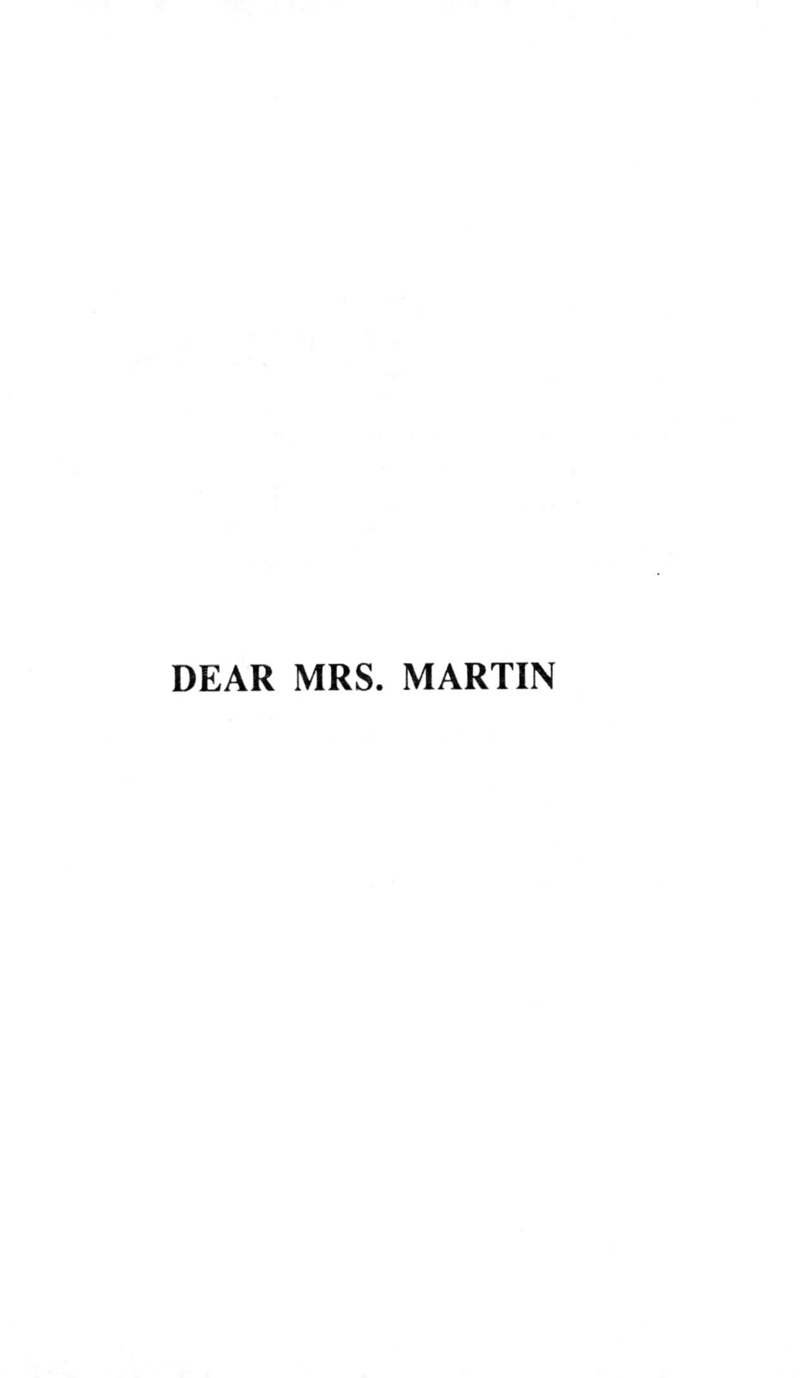

DEAR MRS. MARTIN

Dear Mrs. Martin was first presented at the Iowa Playwrights Festival at the University of Iowa on May 2,1991. It was directed by Rebecca Gilman. Douglas Dawson was stage manager; the assistant director was Scott Hixson. Set design was by Dan Nemteanu and costume design by Kerri S. Bradley. The lighting was by Michael Anderson and sound by Robert Handel. The cast was as follows:

GLORIA ....Rachael Lindhart
BARBARA ....Judalyn Martin
HILARY......................Gwendolyn A. Link

CHARACTERS

Gloria—a woman in her mid-forties

Barbara—a woman in her early-to-middle forties

Hilary—Barbara's best friend; a voice on the telephone

TIME & PLACE

The present. It is autumn.
The living room of a large older home.

SCENE ONE—A FRIDAY AFTERNOON

SCENE: The living room of a large older home. Furnishings indicate that the occupants have not only money, but also good taste. A doorway up left opens into a hallway that exits to the outside. An archway up center opens into a dining room and from there into the rest of the house.

The furniture in the living room should include a couch, at least one large chair, a table with a telephone and answering machine, and a small writing table with a chair. The floor is carpeted and there is a hall tree or a closet near the hallway exit.

AT RISE: As the LIGHTS come up, GLORIA is energetically dusting. SHE is wearing blue jeans and a sweatshirt with "World's Greatest Mom" printed on it. A recording of an UPBEAT SONG from the sixties is playing. The carpet is freshly vacuumed; the vacuum is still out. GLORIA is dusting in time to the music.

SHE finishes her dusting and puts her feather duster into a plastic carry-all. SHE turns off the tape player. From her purse, SHE extracts a pen and a pad of notepaper. SHE sits and begins writing. Although SHE quits writing during the monologue and gets up to address the audience, SHE still holds her pen and it is all part of her "letter."

GLORIA. Dear Mr. and Mrs. Martin, (*SHE frowns, tears off the sheet, crumples it into a wad, and stuffs it in her purse.*) Dear Barb and Marty, (*Shakes her head, tears off the sheet, crumples it up, and puts it in her purse. Thinks awhile.*) Hi there! (*Nods, goes on.*) Well, I thought I'd leave you a little note to tell you that you need to get Windex. I do carry some with me but I like to save it for emergencies. (*SHE gets up, starts to pack up her supplies. Stops, sits, and begins writing again.*) I'm glad that I had your house today as it doesn't take me so long as some of the others on account of you folks are so neat I hardly have any work to do. I should give you a discount. HA! (*SHE makes a big exclamation point.*) The reason I'm in such a rush is that my son, Pooch, the middle one, has a football game and I want to see him play. (*Stops writing.*) Last time they lost 54–0. It would have been worse, but the schools have some rule about how you have to stop if one team gets to 50 points. It's a good thing, too, as they were still in the first half. I can't imagine what the score would have been if they hadn't stopped. My husband, Buck, says they couldn't have gone much higher because the scoreboard can't show any more than two numbers for each team. HA! I don't know what that school was thinking of naming their team the Fighting Midgets; I think it gives the other team a psychological advantage. Anyway, Pooch will probably get to play because many of the boys are injured. (*Starts writing.*) Pooch and the others are so worried about getting hurt that they've started having a prayer before every game just like the Catholics do. (*SHE puts the cap on her pen, puts it back in her purse. SHE puts the vacuum away in a closet. Pauses. SHE retrieves the pen from her purse, sits, and begins writing again.*) Not that I have anything against the Catholics, you know. My great aunt Bunny was a nun once. She's from my father's side of the family, that's where the Catholics are. The rest of us are Baptists and proud of it. I remember this poem my grandma taught me:

A Baptist born and a Baptist bred and a Baptist till I die.
And when I die I'll go to heaven and eat all that Baptist pie.

(Stops writing.)

I never knew exactly what a Baptist pie was but she used to recite that poem so much that we all got kind of sick of it. Anyway, Aunt Bunny went off to the convent and they changed her name to Sister Terrance. She only lasted a few months, then she left and traveled all around the Midwest working as a tassel dancer. Do you know what that is? It's pretty amazing. I saw her do it once at a family reunion and I couldn't believe my eyes. My cousin tried to do it and dislocated her shoulder. She says it still hurts but she is able to tell the weather with it now. *(Starts writing.)* Bunny moved to Las Vegas, but she's still a religious person. She plays the organ for seven o'clock mass every morning. Then she goes to a place called "Slots O'Luck" and plays the slot machines all day until it's time for five o'clock mass. HA! *(Gets up, goes to kitchen, comes back with a can of diet soda, and sits.)* I don't think that you are Catholics because I noticed that you have pork chops thawing for supper and it *is* a Friday. I know the Pope said it's okay to eat meat on Friday now but a lot of Catholics who are our age are still in the habit of fish on Fridays.

My oldest son, Buck Jr., is still having his problems. *(Stops writing.)*

Last week he got up on the roof of the high school and wouldn't come down until the shop teacher apologized for making fun of his birdhouse. They called Buck Sr. at work and he had to go there to talk him into coming down. Buck Sr. was pretty mad. When I got home he said, "Well, your son really shit in his mess kit this time." I hope you're not shocked by this but Buck was in the Army for twenty years and sometimes his language is colorful. Besides, I notice that you get letters from *Save the Whales* so I figure that you are liberals. Well, Buck stormed out of the house, but then he came right back. Sometimes he just needs to slam a door or two, then he's okay. He took us all out to dinner at Walt's Chat 'n' Chew; it was catfish night. All you can eat. Buck never could stay mad long. *(Starts writing.)* Well, I've got to get moving. Sometimes Pooch's games don't last very long so I want to be sure to be there for the kickoff. See you next week. Gloria. P.S. I caught your cat eating one of the plants in the family room. Looks like he's been there before. Sometimes they are missing certain vitamins and eat things like people they shouldn't. *(Rereads this, sees her error, and adds punctuation.)* ... and eat things COMMA like people COMMA that they shouldn't. I have a nephew—Buck's side—who eats dirt. Not dirt exactly but clay. At the family picnic he wouldn't eat his food but got down with his spoon and went after a mound of clay instead. Who can figure it? HA! *(SHE gets up and starts to put things away. Goes back to note.)* P.P.S. Don't forget the Windex.

(SHE props the note against a lamp, removes an invisible
fleck of dust from the table with her sleeve, picks up
her purse, tape player, and cleaning supplies, takes one

last look at the room, and exits. The LIGHTS fade out. In the BLACKOUT, there is the BEEP from a telephone answering machine and HILARY'S VOICE is heard.)

HILARY. Hi, Barbie. It's Hilary! Listen, I called earlier and got your cleaning woman. Is she supposed to be answering the phone? You'd better get that straightened out; it's important that *someone* be in charge. I just hope you screened this one carefully. Marcia Tillinghast had a cleaning woman who stole all of their Hummels. Every last one—even the apple tree boy. She replaced them all with cheap replicas and was halfway to Mexico before Marcia discovered that the goose girl had "Made in Taiwan" stamped on her tush. I know it must be hard for you to have to replace Inez. After all she was with your family for years. I hope this new one works out just as well. Be careful, Barbie. Sometimes you and Marty are just a smitch too trusting. Anyway, call me when you get home. We need to talk about this week's bridge game. See you!

SCENE TWO—THE NEXT WEEK

LIGHTS come up to reveal BARBARA seated at the table and writing. BARBARA is in her early fifties, immaculately groomed and fashionably dressed. SHE is dressed for work and her briefcase is open on the table next to her. The morning NEWS is heard in the background.

BARBARA. Dear Gloria, I bought more Windex. You will find it in the cupboard under the kitchen sink. Right side. Please let me know if there are more supplies that I should be getting for you. *(SHE stops writing, begins to close her briefcase, stops, and begins writing again.)* I was sorry to hear that your son's team lost another football game. *(Stops writing.)* Marty said to tell him that 49 to 3 is a very ... *(SHE pauses, searching for the right word.)* ... *respectable* score. I hope that your oldest son is feeling better now. Have you considered taking him to a doctor? I have left your check on the dining room table. Have a nice day. Barbara Martin. *(SHE begins to leave. Picks up briefcase. Stops and goes back to note.)* P.S. Perhaps it would be better if you did not answer our phone while you are here. *(SHE puts the note down and starts to walk away. Glances back at note then goes back and adds:)* I don't want you to feel that we are taking advantage of your services.

(LIGHTS fade out.)

SCENE THREE—LATER THE SAME DAY

LIGHTS come up on GLORIA. SHE has finished her cleaning and her letter. SHE is seated at the table and is reading the letter aloud, occasionally correcting punctuation. SHE is wearing a red sweatshirt with "MIDGETS" emblazoned across the front.

GLORIA ... so I said to him, apologize to your brother for hitting him with the frozen waffles and let me get back to my work! I suppose school vacation days are nice for the kids, but they sure are hell on the parents. HA!

How nice of you to notice the results of Pooch's last game. They probably wouldn't have scored at all if it hadn't been for Mother Nature. Do you remember that big storm we had late last Friday? Well, it was getting nasty-looking by the fourth quarter and, just as Wesley Pinkpank was trying to kick his field goal, this huge gust of wind came up. It tore the pom-poms out of the cheerleaders hands and blew the band's bass drummer right over sideways. Drum and all. It also carried the ball far enough to go straight through the goal posts. It was little Wesley's first field goal in two years. His dad, Ottie Pinkpank, ran onto the field and tried to tear down the goal post all by himself. It took the team mascot and the entire trombone section to get him off the field. Quite a moment for the Midgets!

I'm meeting my family at the Leaning Tower of Pizza for tacos, then we're going to the game. Tonight we play Our Lady of Victory. They have such huge players on their team; Buck says it's because the Catholic schools can recruit from all over the city and they pick the biggest kids they can find. Buck Jr. says that he has it on good authority that their quarterback is twenty-seven years old and is on parole. I just hope no one gets hurt. See you next week! Gloria. P.S. Go Midgets!

(SHE raises a determined fist in the air. BLACKOUT.)

SCENE FOUR—THE FOLLOWING
THURSDAY EVENING

BARBARA enters, carrying a glass of wine and her checkbook. SHE is dressed casually in jeans and a sweater. SHE puts on some music—a Brahms sextet. BARBARA crosses to the phone and dials. SHE listens for awhile before speaking:

BARBARA. Hi, Hilary. It's Barbara. I really didn't want anything. Just called to visit. I'll call you tomorrow. (*SHE puts the phone down and looks around the room. SHE crosses to the desk and writes a check. SHE ponders the check for awhile, then picks up her briefcase. SHE removes a legal pad and pen and begins writing.*) Thursday p.m. Dear Gloria, I have to be at work earlier than usual tomorrow, so I thought I would write a quick note to you this evening. I have a breakfast meeting with a client who wants to redesign his office and give it a "nautical" theme. I can't come right out and tell this man that no one wants an accountant whose office looks like the Titanic, so I'll spend most of our meeting hinting about other possibilities. It would be so much simpler to be straightforward about it but being direct isn't exactly my strong point. Besides, his wife has already bought about a hundred yards of fishing net and two very startled-looking mounted fish for the wall.

I was happy to read in the paper that your son scored the only touchdown in his game last week. You must be very proud of him. Isn't it hard for you to watch him play? I used to get nervous watching Karen at games—and she was just in the marching band.

Marty is out this evening. Once a month he and his friend, Brandon, go to Brandon's club. After Brandon beats Marty at handball, they have dinner with several old fraternity brothers. He likes Brandon, but he hates the club. Marty's idea of the perfect evening is to sit at home with a big bowl of popcorn and watch an old Jimmy Stewart movie. We probably do scenes from *Shenandoah* in our sleep!

We go out often enough, but we would both rather stay at home. It seems like I spent most of my childhood being dressed up and paraded around in public. My mother and grandmother were always hauling me off to a charity auction or a fashion show or some other event that I cared nothing about. I am sure that they did not intend to make a homebody out of me, but that was certainly what happened. It may sound corny, but I would rather be with my husband and kids than with all the Junior Leaguers in the world.

I hear Marty pulling into the garage, so I'll stop for tonight. Thank you for your fine work; you are *really* doing an excellent job. My regards to your family. Barbara Martin. (*SHE puts down the note and pen and stands. To herself.*) I suppose I'd better get the popcorn started.

(*SHE exits as the LIGHTS fade out.*)

SCENE FIVE—THE NEXT DAY

GLORIA is vacuuming. SHE is wearing headphones and is singing loudly—and off key—to the song on the tape. SHE quits vacuuming, turns off the cassette player, and puts the vacuum away. SHE goes to the kitchen, returns with a soda, sits, and begins writing.

GLORIA. Dear *(Tentatively.)* Barbara. Thank you for the nice note and your kind thoughts about Pooch. He was thrilled to score the touchdown even though it didn't quite happen as they had planned. *(Stops writing.)* One of those big boys from the other team shoved Pooch just as he caught a pass. He stumbled, got his cleats caught in his pants, and did a sort of one-handed cartwheel right over the goal line. Nobody could believe that the Midgets had actually scored a touchdown. The coach started crying and ran up to the stands to hug his wife. Our youngest got so excited that he fell back off the bleachers and hung there by his knees until Buck Sr. could pull him back up. It was a madhouse! The boys from the team gave Pooch the game ball. They let them take it right up to his hospital room to give it to him. Oh, I guess I forgot to tell you that part, didn't I? Well, it seems that the others got so excited about the touchdown that they just piled on top of Pooch and broke his leg. It's a terrible thing to see your child carried off the field on a stretcher, but Pooch was so happy that he just smiled and waved to the crowd all the way to the ambulance. People tore up their popcorn boxes and made confetti to throw as he went past. It was almost like that parade they had to welcome home John Glenn.

You know, when he was little, Buck Jr. told everyone that *he* wanted to be an astronaut. One day I came home to find that he had wrapped his entire body in aluminum foil. He thought it looked like a spacesuit. Actually he looked more like a gigantic baked potato. HA! The foil all fell off, but for a solid week he would only drink Tang and eat beef jerky. He said that was what the astronauts ate.

We were glad when that phase was over. I don't suppose that your kids ever did anything *that* strange, did they?

My psychic told me that she thinks Buck Jr. was some kind of explorer in another life. Maybe a Viking. She believes that his spirit is anxious to roam again and that's why he seems so unsettled. She also told me that Buck Sr. and I are soul mates and are starting our fourth life together. At first I had trouble believing this but I do have this dream from time to time where I'm in ancient Rome and it's burning all around me and there is some man in a chariot who saves me. I never thought much about it because I only have the dream after we've been to The Tired Texan for dinner. But it seems so real. Maybe the man in the chariot is Buck.

Speaking of romance, I couldn't help but notice the flowers in the dining room. Must be some special occasion, like an anniversary. This year for our anniversary, Buck took me for a cruise on that riverboat where they have music and dancing. We've never been ones for big parties, so this was perfect. It was wonderful and *very* romantic. Buck even took a Dramamine just so that we could go.

Last month we went to Buck's sister's wedding anniversary. Twenty-five years. They handed out these big, red hearts that said, "Billy and Eva, Twenty-five Years" in fancy, silver letters. I couldn't even figure out what it was supposed to be until Buck said that they were refrigerator magnets. Can you imagine? Handing out refrigerator magnets for your anniversary? I found it a little tacky, but Billy is in the advertising specialties business, so I suppose he got a deal on them. Buck says maybe they'll do bumper stickers for their fiftieth. HA!

Well, happy whatever! Gloria.

(SHE stops writing, props the note against the lamp. SHE gathers up her supplies and the LIGHTS fade. In the BLACKOUT, the answering machine BEEPS.)

HILARY. Barbie. It's Hilary. Just called to see if I could borrow your punch bowl for our anniversary party. The caterer doesn't think that we need another one, but I don't want anything to go wrong. This party is just going to be the best ever. I was going to keep this a secret, but we have the cutest favors for everyone. You'll never guess what they are! Here's a hint. You'll remember us every time you go to the fridge! Got to run. Bye.

SCENE SIX—THE FOLLOWING FRIDAY

BARBARA is seated at the table, writing to Gloria. SHE is dressed for work and drinking a cup of coffee.

BARBARA. Dear Gloria, You were right, it was our anniversary. Twenty-three years. Marty had a singing telegram delivered to my office. It was an Elvis impersonator singing the first song that Marty and I ever danced to. The singer was really dreadful and Elvis never recorded that song anyway—but the singing telegram place only had Elvis or something called Beefsteak, the Singing Tomato available, so Marty decided that Elvis might be better. Actually, since it's "our song" it didn't really make much difference who sang it. It always sounds good to me.

So sorry to hear about Pooch. Marty says to tell him not to worry, a lot of players get injured and then come back stronger than ever. You'll notice a package on the dining room table. Marty would like for you to give it to Pooch. It's a football, autographed by Gale Sayers. This is evidently of some significance to football fans, but I'm afraid that I don't know what it is. Anyway, Marty has treasured it for years. Neither of our kids have much of an interest in sports, so Marty would like for Pooch to have it. He said it sounds like Pooch earned it.

What hospital is Pooch in? Marty works at St. Ludmilla's and said that he'd like to stop in to visit him. Our kids always tease Marty and tell him that the hospital doesn't get its money's worth out of him as an administrator because he spends all his time with the patients.

You asked if my children ever went through any unusual phases. Plenty of them, believe me. When John was eight, he was fascinated by Superman. So, his aunt got him a little Superman costume for his birthday. John put it on immediately, went outside, and tried to fly over the maple tree in the back yard. He knocked himself unconscious and had to have ten stitches in his forehead. John was so upset by the whole thing that Marty spent hours rigging up a special harness and pulley in the tree so that John could actually fly. I wish I had a photograph of them—John with his little arms straight out in front of him, looking so serious. And Marty in the background, soaked with sweat, his face bright red, working his hardest to make John's dream come true. It's one of my most precious memories.

Marty and I have been lucky; our kids have always been good. Not perfect certainly, but I never wanted for them to be perfect. I think if I had my childhood to live over, I'd do it differently. Ask more questions, let myself get dirty, have more friends who weren't out of the same cookie cutter that I was. I think I misbehaved *once* as a teenager. When I was sixteen, I painted the face of my grandmother's lawn jockey white. She was furious, but she never found out who did it. I was disappointed that no one suspected me, but I never told a soul. Until Marty.

I hope that you are all well. My best wishes to your family. Barbara. P.S. I have never seen a psychic, but I know what you mean about being Buck's soul mate. It's the same way with Marty. I feel like he knows me by heart.

(LIGHTS fade out.)

SCENE SEVEN—LATER THE SAME AFTERNOON

GLORIA is seated in a chair, her eyes closed, listening to a self-help tape. Her cleaning is finished and her supplies are already packed up and waiting by the door, SHE is repeating affirmations after the voice on the tape.

TAPE. I am relaxed and at peace with my universe.

GLORIA. I am relaxed and at peace with my universe.

TAPE. All good things are coming to me easily and effortlessly.

GLORIA. All good things are coming to me easily and effortlessly.

TAPE. I now recognize, accept, and follow the cosmic plan for my life as it is revealed to me step by step.

GLORIA. I now recognize, accept, and follow the cosmic plan for ... for, oh, what was that? The cosmic plan is revealed ... I follow the recognized plan ... oh, to hell with it.

TAPE. Now imagine that the energy is gathering at your feet, and let it flow slowly up through the center of your body from your feet to your head.

(GLORIA follows the instructions on the tape.)

TAPE. The energy radiates from the top of your head like a fountain of light, then flows back down the outside of your body to your feet. Now slowly open your eyes and become as one with your surroundings. Perfectly relaxed, centered, and open.

(GLORIA opens her eyes and slowly gets up from the chair. SHE takes several deep "cleansing" breaths, then goes to the kitchen and comes back with a glass of water. GLORIA sits at the table and begins her note.)

GLORIA. Dear Barbara. Your husband came home from work early today, just as I was finishing up. I guess he isn't feeling well. We chatted for awhile, then he went to take a nap and I haven't heard a peep out of him since. Luckily I was done with the vacuuming, so I don't think that I disturbed him. I really enjoyed our little chat. He seems like such a kind man. He was so very thoughtful and asked how Pooch was getting along. He seemed quite tickled when I told him that Pooch was not only delighted with the football, but has made a little shrine for it in his hospital room. Pooch *is* in St. Ludmilla's, so your husband said that he'll stop by tomorrow and have lunch with him.

I told him to be careful with that cold. My youngest, Beanie, has had one for a week now and the doctor said that it can turn into pneumonia just like that. Have your husband repeat this twenty times every morning: "I am aglow with good health."

(SHE closes her eyes, takes a deep breath, and whispers the affirmation to herself a few times.)

My great-aunt, Hildy, used to say that the only way to cure a cold was to put a fish head and seven cloves of garlic in a wool scarf and tie it around your chest. She was an odd one, Hildy. Odd and bad-smelling, as I recall.

Anyway, I have been learning a lot about the power of visualization in my life. Lady Diantha, my psychic, tells me that I can make any changes in myself that I want through affirmations, visualization, and the cleansing of my body. Buck says that I will believe anything that she tells me but that it is my own money so I can spend it however I like. Besides, she has been right about everything so far. Today I noticed that she had changed her sign from "Psychic" to "Holistic Practitioner and Spiritual Guide." I'm not sure what that means, but I intend to keep seeing her.

I hope that your husband is feeling himself again soon.

(Rereads this, frowns, make corrections, and reads again.)

I hope that your husband is feeling *like* himself again soon.

Sorry to be so brief today, but we are having someone come to paint our garage. He is a friend of ours who has been having trouble finding work so we have been trying to help him out with a few odd jobs. He put a new front door on for us last weekend. By Monday, we couldn't get it to close tightly and by Tuesday one of the hinges was coming off. I guess it's no wonder he has trouble finding work. HA!

Take care of your husband. And yourself. And try to stay in white light. It is the healing light, you know. Gloria.

(SHE stops writing, props the note against the lamp. SHE exits into the kitchen to return her water glass. As she exits, the PHONE rings. GLORIA enters, begins to answer the phone, then stops herself. The message begins and GLORIA listens to it.)

HILARY. Barbie. Hil. I dropped by your house this afternoon to return your punch bowl. When I got to the front door, I just peeked into your living room window and saw—what's her name? Gloria?—all stretched out in your chair like she owned the place. She had her eyes closed and it looked like she was talking to herself. Barbs, have you checked your medicine cabinet lately? Deborah Winslow had a cleaning woman who took her Valium and filled the bottles up with Tic-Tacs. Maybe I could send Brandon over some time when she's there. To check her out. I just couldn't bring myself to ring the bell, I was afraid she might be violent. You know how they get when they're all hopped up like that. You two just be careful. I'll bring your punch bowl back some other day. Bye.

(GLORIA begins to exit and stops.)

GLORIA. Ha!

BLACKOUT

SCENE EIGHT—EVENING, THE SAME DAY

BARBARA enters, she has just gotten home from work.

BARBARA. Marty, I'm home!

(SHE takes her shoes off and sprawls on the chair. SHE begins reading the note from Gloria.)

BARBARA. Beanie? What were we thinking when we gave our kids names like John and Karen? (*Reads on.*) I wonder if our HMO covers Holistic Practitioners?

God, I would love to see the look on Mother's face if I told her I had an appointment with my psychic! (*Speaks into imaginary phone.*) So sorry, Mother, can't do lunch. Lady Diantha is taking me back to the sixteenth century today. (*Laughs and reads on.*) I am aglow with good health? Marty, did you read this? Gloria has a cure for your cold. (*SHE shrugs. SHE goes on reading, stops, looks to see if Marty is coming, then closes her eyes and begins reciting the affirmation.*) I am aglow with good health. I am aglow with good health. I am … Marty? What are you doing?

(*BARBARA gets up and exits into the kitchen as the LIGHTS fade out.*)

SCENE NINE—ONE WEEK LATER

LIGHTS come up to reveal both BARBARA and GLORIA on stage. THEY stand about four feet apart. The stage is dimly lit except for pools of LIGHT on EACH WOMAN.

GLORIA. Dear Barbara. Don't worry about the messy house. That's my department. You just need to take care of yourself and leave the house to me. I know that you are used to being strong but it's okay now to let others be strong for you.

BARBARA. Dear Gloria, How thoughtful of you to send the lovely basket of fruit. We all appreciated it. Thank you for coming a few days early. With so many people coming and going, the place has really gotten to be a mess.

GLORIA. My father told me a week before he died to take all of his dishes, sheets, towels, everything. He said he was moving. I told him he would need those things and he said he was going where it was all provided.

BARBARA. I cannot even begin to imagine my life without Marty. We are so much a part of one another. We met in high school and we could tell, even then, that we were meant to be together. I never dated another boy after I met Marty.

GLORIA. The few times I met Marty I really liked him. He was a very good man, Barbara. He loved you and your children very much. I was so sad to hear about his passing, but I also know that one day I will see his smiling face on the other side and it gives me peace to know that I have a friend waiting there for me.

BARBARA. People say to me, "You're so lucky. You had twenty-three wonderful years together." But you know, Gloria, I don't feel so damn lucky. I'm greedy, I admit it. I wanted sixty more.

GLORIA. I never would get close to people because of the hurt involved with losing them. But I have been allowed to see and hear things that most people cannot. I have seen the steps to heaven.

BARBARA. We were already starting to plan our vacation for next summer ...

GLORIA. I had surgery once and nearly died. I had the gift of seeing the other side.

BARBARA. I don't know about the cars. I don't know about getting the licenses, or when to have the tires rotated...

GLORIA. I know that the spirit does separate from the body.

BARBARA. Our New Year's Eve dinner party ...

GLORIA.The spirit feels no pain and it has all the wisdom and peace that heaven can offer.

BARBARA. I can't reach the top shelf in our bedroom closet ...

GLORIA. The spirit can move with a blink of the eye from one place to another.

BARBARA. I have never slept in that bed without him...

GLORIA. The spirit at death usually comes back home and looks around. For three days, it will travel to all the places where it felt good, like old homes, the school it went to, anyplace that it has fond memories. Buck's dad's spirit stayed for five years until his mother remarried. That's why people who lose an arm or a leg can still feel it. It's always there. My uncle, Whitey, lost an arm in World War I. Well, not exactly *in* the war. He always talked about getting hurt in the war, so we just assumed he'd been fighting in it. It turns out that he got drunk and fell off a train somewhere in Kentucky on his way to being shipped out.

(LIGHTS begin to fade slowly.)

Now, Buck's cousin, Buster, really did get hurt in the war. Actually, he's not really his cousin, he is the son of

Buck's mother's cousin so I guess that would make them second cousins, or is it first cousins twice removed ...?

(In the BLACKOUT, the answering machine BEEPS. It is HILARY, who sounds very tentative and uncomfortable.)

HILARY. Barbie? It's Hilary. And Brandon. We just called to say what a lovely service it was. Just what Marty would have wanted ... I guess. The flowers were lovely and the music was beautiful. Was that "Shenandoah" that they played at the beginning? I didn't think so, but Brandon swore that it was. We sent the peach roses. I hope you saw them. Take care and stay in touch. We love you.

(The machine BEEPS again. This time it is GLORIA. BARBARA enters as Gloria's speech begins. SHE is wearing faded jeans and a man's bathrobe.)

GLORIA. Hello, Barbara. This is Gloria calling to say that I got your message. No, it wouldn't upset my schedule to skip your house again this week. And don't even think about paying me! I only expect to be paid for the work I do, not for work that I don't do. Are you sure you don't want me to stop by for a little while? I wouldn't have to do the whole job, just tidy up a bit. I could stop by around ten...

(BARBARA switches off the answering machine. SHE looks at the machine for a while, then goes to the desk, sits, and takes out her pad and pen.)

Dear Gloria. Thank you ... (*BARBARA crosses out what she has written and thinks awhile before continuing.*) Please ... Damn! (*BARBARA again crosses out what she has written.*) I am so ... (*BARBARA puts down her pen.*) I am so *what*? So miserable? So exhausted? So terrified? So alone.

(*BARBARA sits staring straight ahead as the LIGHTS fade out. In the BLACKOUT, the answering machine BEEPS.*)

HILARY. Barbie. It's Hilary. I'm sorry that I haven't called sooner. I just thought that maybe you'd like to be left alone for awhile. I can't imagine what this must be like for you, but maybe it's not good to be moping around. Maybe you should go on a trip or something. Are you planning to stay in the house? Brandon and I drove by last week. It didn't look like you were home, so we didn't stop. I noticed that your leaves are really starting to pile up. You don't want to upset your neighbors by letting the house get run down, do you? Call me and I'll give you the name of my yard man.

Well, I have to run. The Mindermans are coming over for bridge and I haven't even started ... Oh. I hope you don't feel left out. I know the four of us played together for years; I just thought it might make you sad. And I wasn't sure who to get for a fourth and ... Well, I know you understand. Call me if you need anything. I'm your best friend and I'll be right here for you.

SCENE TEN—ONE MONTH LATER

(BARBARA is seated at the table. SHE is dressed for work, although SHE looks slightly rumpled and somehow less well-arranged than in prior scenes. SHE is drinking a cup of coffee and writing to Gloria.)

BARBARA. Dear Gloria. Well, I have somehow survived my first week back at work. People there are generally quite understanding and kind. It is obvious that a few of them don't know what to say to me, so they don't say anything at all. I find that very painful. My friend, Hilary, usually manages to say the wrong thing, but at least she speaks to me. Or, rather, to my answering machine.

It has been nice to be busy. It is so hard to come home to this house and know that Marty's not here. Sometimes, when I see his car in the driveway, I play a little game and pretend that he *is* here, waiting to surprise me. Then I come into this big house and realize that it is as empty as I am.

I have gone out every night this week. Once with a friend who lost her husband five years ago. Lost. Why do people say that? It's not as though Marty just turned up missing one day. Anyway, this woman's husband *died* five years ago. We went to Ludlow's Family Cafeteria. Do you know that place? "Cookin' Like Mom's at a Price Dad Will Love." There were just a few people there. Most of them hunched over their food eating alone.

Oh, God, is this what I have to look forward to?

After we left there, I went to a movie. Sat through two showings of the same film. It wasn't a very good movie—

something about a bunch of teenagers who spent hours driving around in their father's car—but at least it kept me occupied.

Last night Hilary and Brandon took me out to dinner. They really don't know what to say to me either so they talked about silly things. Brandon spent hours telling me about his research on adolescent acne and Hilary gave me a rundown on the personal lives of all of her neighbors. If you have any questions about Bitsy Bergstrom and her unfortunate face-lift, just ask away. I feel as though I'm an expert on the subject now.

I know that Brandon and Hilary try—and this must be hard for them too. Marty and Brandon went to college together; we've known them for years. They mean well, but they do the oddest things. The week after Marty died they sent me several laminated copies of his obituary. What in the world am I supposed to do? Use them for bookmarks?

Anyway, last night I wanted to tell Hilary and Brandon to either shut up or talk about something that mattered. But it's always been hard for me to say what I'm feeling. I guess I'm afraid of hurting someone or making them angry. My grandmother always said that a lady knows when to bite her tongue. After all these years, I'm surprised that I have any tongue left.

Must run. See you next Friday. Barbara. P.S. Do you have any idea how my leaves got raked?

SCENE ELEVEN—AFTERNOON, THE SAME DAY

LIGHTS come up on GLORIA, who is seated at the table, polishing silver. A sixties tune is playing. GLORIA is humming along. SHE finishes her polishing and exits with the silver and the polishing supplies. SHE comes back into the room and turns off the tape. SHE crosses to the table, takes out her pad and pen, sits, and begins writing.

GLORIA. Dear Barbara. Well, I should have known better than to even go out of the house today. Friday the thirteenth is always bad for me. Not that I'm terribly superstitious, you know. I don't walk under ladders and all the normal things, but I'm not overly superstitious. Not like my cousin, Mary Fay. She's an identical twin; her sister is named Fairy May. Can you believe that? (*Stops writing.*) Anyway, Mary Fay is so superstitious she can barely get out of the house. When we were kids, it used to take us forty-five minutes to walk from Grandma's house to the Hinky Dinky. It was only five blocks away, but Mary Fay had to be careful not to step on any cracks. Well, a few years ago she was on her way to her sister's wedding and a black cat started to cross the road in front of her. So, she slammed on the brakes, backed up and drove about twenty miles out of her way just to avoid that cat's path. She was half an hour late to Fairy May's wedding and Fairy was furious. So, after the honeymoon, Fairy went over to Mary's house when she wasn't home.

She put an open ladder over every door to the house. Mary got home, saw those ladders, and drove her station wagon right through the garage and into the family room. She claimed that Fairy caused her to have bad luck and Fairy said that Mary was too dumb to watch where she was going and that she couldn't take a joke. Anyway, they haven't spoken now for several years. I think they should forget about it. There was no permanent harm done, and Mary's husband was able to put in a very lovely fireplace in the hole in the family room.

Actually, it's not just Friday the thirteenth that's been bad. It's been like this the whole week. On Monday, we got a note from Beanie's teacher saying that he couldn't eat lunch with the other kids the rest of this week. Seems he had been making nose prints in his Jello. So he has had to bring his own lunch all week. I let him make it the first day, until I discovered that he had packed three cans of root beer, an entire bag of marshmallows, and a peanut butter and Nestles Quik sandwich. Good old Mom took over after that.

Then on Wednesday I had to rush Buck Jr. to the orthodontist. He got his braces caught in the volleyball net during PE and it took the school nurse thirty minutes to cut him loose.

This morning was the topper though. I had to go pick up our dry cleaning. I had on a wrap-around denim skirt and when I left the cleaners, it blew off. I am not kidding, it just blew right off. I had my hands full of cleaning, so I just calmly walked to the car. My coat was in the back seat, so I put it on and retrieved my skirt. I don't know if anyone saw me; I tried to look like it was perfectly normal to stroll around town in my pink-flowered underpants. On the way home, I stopped and put that skirt in the Goodwill drop box. Who needs to go through that again?

Well, that's enough about me. I think it is great that you went back to work and that you are keeping busy. Just don't keep too busy.

I saw Lady Diantha last week. She said that my future looks promising and fruitful. Then she looked sort of surprised and asked me what I did for a living. I told her that I was in toilets and hadn't found any gold in them 'thar holes yet. HA! I do love my work though. I had a chance to go work for Buck's sister. Maybe you've seen her store over on Smoking Oak Road? It's called Eva's Unique Antique Boutique. It's a cute little shop, but I just couldn't stand the thought of being cooped up in one place all day. This way I work someplace different every day, I am pretty much my own boss, and I get to provide a service to people like you. I couldn't ask for anything better!

I took the liberty of talking to Lady Diantha about you. She says that she sees you clothed in a robe of light, protected and guided through life. She said to remember that life is a gift that needs to be cherished, loved, and enjoyed. It probably doesn't seem that way now, but in time it will. Right now, you just need to let yourself feel. I think it is great to keep active and busy, but don't deny yourself the chance to really feel whatever is there to feel. If you feel sad, cry. Cry until your head hurts and your eyes are swollen. If you're angry, beat on a pillow. Go outside and throw rocks at the moon. But whatever you're feeling, let it out. Let yourself feel, Barbara.

See you next week. Your friend, Gloria. P.S. I thought you might be too tired to fix a proper dinner, so I made a nice little spinach salad for you. It's in the refrigerator. I noticed the Hilary and Brandon refrigerator magnet was gone. Is it missing?

BLACKOUT

SCENE TWELVE—EARLY EVENING, THE SAME DAY

BARBARA enters. SHE looks exhausted as SHE puts down her briefcase, takes off her coat, picks up Gloria's note, and slowly goes to the answering machine. SHE pushes the button and hears two messages, the first from HILARY and the second from GLORIA. When SHE hears that it is Hilary on the machine, SHE crosses to the table and begins reading Gloria's note while HILARY talks.

HILARY. Barbie. I feel as your friend I must tell you this. This morning I was on my way to have my nails done. I drove by that little mini-mall over on Weeping Willow Drive. You know the one I mean? Anyway, I saw that Gloria person, the one who works for you. She was carrying somebody's dry cleaning. Not her own, I'm sure. She seems more like the wash and wear type. *(Laughs.)* I certainly hope that you can take this, Barbie, but she was wearing only her underwear. And she was walking along like there was nothing out of the ordinary about being out in public in her lingerie. I am sorry to be the one to tell you this. God knows, you don't need anymore troubles after all you've been through. But I thought that you needed to know what kind of person is in your house every Friday. I warned you about the drug business and you didn't seem concerned. But Barbie, this woman is a pervert. What if she is some sort of a lesbian? If you don't have the heart to fire her, call Brandon. He'll be glad to do it for you. We just don't want anyone to take advantage of you. Call me!

GLORIA. Hello, Barbara. It's me. Gloria. I am such a flake this week, I can't believe it. Do you ever feel that way? You know, when you push the button to close the garage door and then drive away and once you are out of sight you wonder if you did, so you drive around the block to make sure and find out it was closed all along but by then you are ten minutes late to wherever you're going? Anyway, I think I forgot my tape player at your house. I have tapes that I listen to when I work, mostly old songs from the '60s. I like that music, it's energetic and makes my cleaning go so quickly. I'll stop by tomorrow to pick it up. Have a good evening and remember my advice.

(BARBARA looks around the room, finds the tape player, and turns it on. SHE listens to the end of the song that Gloria was playing and half-heartedly dances around the room. When the song finishes, another slower number comes on. It is apparent that this is Barbara and Marty's "song." SHE quickly moves to turn it off, but then stops and lets it play. SHE goes to the hall tree near the door and removes Marty's jacket. SHE bunches it up, holds it to her face, and inhales deeply. Then SHE holds the arm of the jacket in one hand, drapes the other arm over her shoulder, and begins dancing with the jacket as the LIGHTS fade slowly to BLACK. The MUSIC slowly fades in the blackout. The answering machine BEEPS and HILARY is heard.)

HILARY. Barbie? Hi, it's Hil. I just realized that I still have your punch bowl. Actually it came in handy. I had a little birthday brunch for Brandon yesterday, so I used it to make the Mimosas. I hope you don't mind. Why haven't we heard from you, dear? Brandon says these depressions are normal but he thinks you should be snapping out of it. He knows a good psychiatrist, Jason Upton, who could prescribe something to make you ...

(LIGHTS come up on BARBARA, who has picked up the telephone.)

BARBARA. Hilary? It's Barbara. Barbara, Hilary. Not Barbs. And definitely not Barbie. Now please be quiet and listen to what I have to say. Please don't call me until you are able to talk about something that matters. You have no class, Hilary. You are not my best friend; my best friend is dead. And, believe it or not, my closest friend is into toilets. Oh, and Hil? Shove that damn punch bowl. *(SHE hangs up. After a moment, SHE looks up smiling.)* HA!

SCENE THIRTEEN—SIX MONTHS LATER

Both BARBARA and GLORIA are on stage. Again, EACH reads her own letters, but this time THEY face one another and respond to the other's letter.

GLORIA. Dear Barbara. Welcome back from sunny Mexico! It's nice that you and your children can enjoy traveling together.

BARBARA. Dear Gloria. Mexico was wonderful. We used to go to Hawaii on our family trips, but we decided that it was time to start some new traditions.

GLORIA. Lady Diantha has time to see you next week. Wednesday is best for her because she is in a bowling league on Thursdays.

BARBARA. You were right; Lady Diantha is amazing. I have already started listening to the tapes she gave me. *(Takes a deep breath.)* I release the past and allow time to heal each part of my life.

GLORIA. No, I don't think it's a bad thing that you sold Marty's car. You can't drive two cars at once anyway.

BARBARA. I am open and accepting of all that the world brings me.

GLORIA. Pooch had to write an essay called "My Most Prized Possession." He wrote about the football that Marty gave him.

BARBARA. I feel the energy of the universe radiating through my whole being.

GLORIA. You are so brave to start running! I can barely walk most of the time. I've signed up to take an aquasize class. It's at 6:30 in the morning, but I figure at that hour no one will really notice how I look in a swimsuit. HA!

BARBARA. I accept all the feelings I'm having as part of myself.

GLORIA. I'm glad that you felt you could call me the other night. You're bound to have some bad times now and then. And it doesn't matter how late it was; you're not going to wake up any of *my* family. One time the house next door to us had a gas leak and exploded and Buck and the boys slept right through it.

BARBARA. I flow with the changes taking place in my life.

GLORIA. You are making your own way, Barbara, and I cheer you on every day.

BARBARA. I approve of myself and the way I'm changing. I am doing the best I can.

BLACKOUT

COSTUMES

Scene One
Gloria: Blue jeans, sweatshirt with "World's Greatest Mom" imprinted on it. Tennis shoes.
Scene Two
Barbara: Jacket, pleated skirt, blouse, heels.
Scene Three
Gloria: Sweatpants, sweatshirt with "MIDGETS" imprinted on it. Tennis shoes.
Scene Four
Barbara: Sweater, blouse, khakis, and flats.
Scene Five
Gloria: Cotton shirt, pants, tennis shoes.
Scene Six
Barbara: Business suit, white shirt, heels.
Scene Seven
Gloria: Two-piece athletic suit, tennis shoes.
Scene Eight
Barbara: Same suit as in Scene Six.
Scene Nine
Barbara: Same suit as in Scenes Six and Eight.
Second entrance-jeans, slippers, and a man's bathrobe.
Gloria: Plaid shirt, khakis, loafers.
Scene Ten
Barbara: Cardigan sweater, blouse, pants, flats.
Scene Eleven
Gloria: Long-sleeved, cotton t-shirt, khakis, tennis shoes.
Scene Twelve
Barbara: Same as Scene Ten.
Scene Thirteen
Barbara: Sweater, turtleneck, pants from previous scene.
Gloria: Sweater, T-shirt, khakis, loafers.

PROPERTY PLOT

Vacuum
Feather duster
Plastic carry-all with cleaning supplies
Purse
Pens (2)
Pads of writing paper (2)
Can of soda (2)
Tape player
Briefcase
Glass of wine
Checkbook
Headphones and personal cassette player
Cup of coffee (2)
Glass of water
Silver
Silver polish
Polishing cloth
Man's jacket

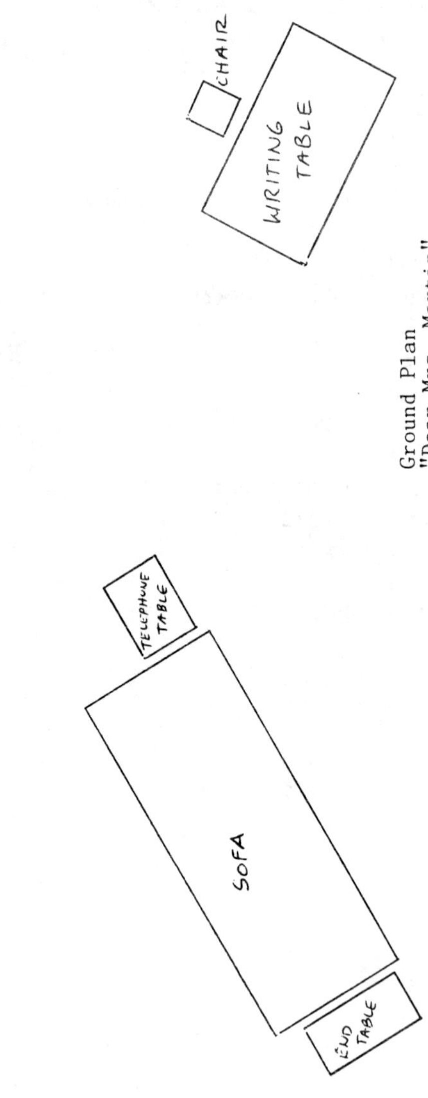

Ground Plan
"Dear Mrs. Martin"

MOTHER'S DAY

For Janet

CHARACTERS

Victoria—a woman of thirty-five

Gail—Victoria's cousin; a year or two older than Victoria
Mary—Victoria's adoptive mother; in her early sixties

Esther—Victoria's birth mother; in her early fifties

The voice of Mrs. Ryan, a social worker, is recorded.

TIME

The present. It is spring.

SCENE: The set consists of several platforms. One long platform downstage is used for the Victoria/Gail scenes and for the telephone scenes. There should be a simple wooden table and chairs and a small cupboard, center, to suggest a kitchen or dining room.

There are two raised platforms, left and right. Each is connected to the downstage platform by separate wooden stairways. The stairways connect to the downstage platform just upstage of the table.

The raised platform, left, is Mary's area; the raised platform, right, is Esther's area.

AT RISE: LIGHTS come up on an empty stage. VICTORIA enters, carrying a small bird in her cupped hands. SHE sits at a table, center, and gently examines the bird.

VICTORIA. Well, it doesn't look like you're hurt. Probably just scared, aren't you? You're pretty tiny to be on your own. *(SHE gets a small box out of a cupboard, lines it with a towel, and puts the bird inside.)* We have a lot in common, you know. I sort of got pushed out of the nest myself. But, at least you remember *your* mom. That's more than I can say.

(SHE gets a bowl and begins mixing together some food— egg yolk, birdseed, chopped raisins—for the bird. GAIL enters.)

GAIL. Hi! Who's the latest refugee? (*GAIL crosses to the table and peers into the box.*)

VICTORIA. A baby robin. I found him at Hawthorne Park. I guess he must have fallen out of the nest. (*VICTORIA holds up the box*) Meet my cousin, Gail.

GAIL. (*Nods to the bird.*) Delighted. (*GAIL looks at the bird closely*). Mr. Welter.

(*VICTORIA looks confused.*)

GAIL. Mr. Welter. Junior high health. He looked just like this, remember? Round head, pointy little beak. Always looking around like he was afraid someone would squash him.

VICTORIA. (*Looks at bird and nods.*) You're right. Mr Welter.

GAIL. Is he hurt?

VICTORIA. Just terrified.

GAIL. Were there any others?

VICTORIA. No, and no sign of Mom either.

GAIL. (*Sits at the table.*) God, he's tinier than those fake birds they put on flower arrangements. The ones with the orange toothpicks for legs. He doesn't have a "Made in Taiwan" sticker on him anyplace, does he?

(*VICTORIA laughs and shakes her head.*)

GAIL. What are you going to do with him? He's a lot smaller than the sparrows you raised last spring.

VICTORIA. Starlings, not sparrows. I'll keep him here and try to feed him. Hope that he'll get strong enough to go out on his own. *(VICTORIA continues mixing the food.)*

GAIL. *(Peering with disgust at food mixture.)* What's that? Looks like somebody already ate it.

VICTORIA. Egg yolk ...

GAIL. *(Covers the top of Mr. Welter's box with her hands.)* Egg yolk! My god! What if it's someone he knows?

VICTORIA. *(Laughs and continues.)* Millet, minced raisins ...

GAIL. The early bird gets the millet? What happened to worms?

VICTORIA. That's when they're older. Or when their mom can chew up a worm and spit it back out for them. I'm not willing to go that far.

GAIL. And you call yourself an animal lover! *(GAIL thinks a moment.)* Bugs, then. Aren't those small enough? He could have a banquet on my privet hedge. Invite all his friends.

VICTORIA. Later—when he's bigger.

GAIL. *(To the robin.)* Odds are you won't ever see *your* mom again, Mr. Welter. Now for your friend here, it's a different story.

(VICTORIA looks puzzled.)

GAIL. Your mailman was just coming up the walk when I got here. You know, they really shouldn't let those guys wear shorts. It was like ... I don't know ... fettucine with boots on. Very unsightly. Anyway, he brought you this. *(GAIL removes an envelope from her jacket pocket and puts it on the table.)* From the State of Ohio.

VICTORIA. My birth certificate? (*VICTORIA picks up the envelope and opens it slowly. SHE withdraws a small folded piece of white paper and looks at it warily.*)

GAIL. Well, who *are* you?

VICTORIA. (*Hands the paper to Gail.*) It's like having somebody send me my own birth announcement.

GAIL. (*Takes the paper and reads a bit before looking up.*) Congratulations! It's a girl!

VICTORIA. What else does it say? What's my mother's name?

GAIL. Well, it seems that you're the first child born to an Esther Louise Peterson, aged, Jesus, aged sixteen, of Watson's Chapel, Ohio.

VICTORIA. Esther. I like that. I was afraid her name would be odd. Winifred or Petunia, or something.

GAIL. You weren't a twin and, great news, you weren't stillborn!

VICTORIA. (*Wads up the envelope and throws it at Gail.*) Smart ass!

GAIL. (*Laughing.*) Hey! You said you wanted me to read it, didn't you? Let's see. You were born on April 27, which we knew, at 4:15 a.m.

VICTORIA. That's all on my other birth certificate. The fake one they make for adoptees. (*SHE gets up and stands behind Gail to look at the birth certificate.*) What about my father?

GAIL. There's a place here for it, but the space is blank.

VICTORIA. Damn. Oh well, I suppose one name is better than none.

GAIL. Don't you think it'll be difficult to track down someone named Peterson? It's not exactly an unusual last name, you know.

VICTORIA. *(Takes the envelope from Gail.)* At least I have a name to go on now. A week ago I didn't even have that. Besides, how many people do you suppose could live in a place called Watson's Chapel? *(Pause. VICTORIA looks over the birth certificate.)*

GAIL. Look, are you sure you want to go through with this?

VICTORIA. Am I *sure*?

GAIL. Vic, you know how I feel about your mother. She's never been just my aunt. God, I always felt like *I* was adopted. Mother and I have never had anything in common. She was always off volunteering somewhere, making the world a better place. It was your mom who took me to my cello lessons, taught me to swim, bought me my first bra; all the mother/daughter memories I have are with your mom, not mine. If she knew that you were looking for this woman, she'd be devastated.

(LIGHTS fade on GAIL. VICTORIA crosses downstage.)

VICTORIA. I was home alone one day when I was thirteen. I don't know what got me going, but I started looking around in my parents' dresser. I poked around under my dad's socks, my mom's nightgowns, looking for *something*. Something adult, forbidden. Secret.

I sure found what I was looking for.

There was an old, brown file folder at the bottom of one of the drawers. It was long, legal-sized, and it smelled like the lavender scented paper that my mom used to line the drawers. Inside were these very important-looking documents that said how this deserving young couple—my parents—were going to take this poor unwanted child—me—into their home and raise her as their own. Well, naturally, I was pretty shocked. All along I thought I *was* their own child and then I find out they were just doing what some judge told them to do.

So, I tried to think back, to find some clues. I remembered some hushed conversations between my mother and my aunt. Whispers that faded when I entered a room. All along I thought it was some grown-up thing that I couldn't know because I was too young. Some family secret I could learn about when I came of age.

Turns out I *was* the family secret.

(LIGHTS fade on VICTORIA as they come up on MARY, Victoria's adoptive mother, upstage left.)

MARY. We honestly meant to tell her. First, we thought she was too young to understand. Then, when she was older, we moved to a new town and we thought we'd wait until she made new friends, got used to her new school. Then she had an appendectomy, her grandmother died, her puppy ran away, her best friend moved. The longer we waited, the easier it got to put it off. *(Turns toward Victoria.)*

You need to understand that it was different then; people weren't as open as they are now. Even the social worker said not to tell you.

(The voice of MRS. RYAN, the social worker, is heard.)

MRS. RYAN. One couple I worked with told their son he was adopted. From the time he was a baby. Oh, they made a *real* big deal of it. Felt it was in his best interest, whatever that means. And do you know what happened? The day he turned eighteen he hitchhiked to Utah and met his real mother. Stayed with her for a month and went to visit her twice a year after that. Well, it broke his poor mother's heart.

She never was the same after that—took to having crying spells and wandering around in the neighbors' houses when they weren't home. Her husband had to put her in a mental facility; then he divorced her and ran off with some high school girl who sold snow cones at the children's zoo.

MARY. Mrs. Ryan, I don't see how this ...

MRS. RYAN. Mary, I'm the expert. Just trust me. You've been through so much; you don't want to jeopardize that, do you?

(LIGHTS fade out on MARY and up on VICTORIA and GAIL. VICTORIA is dialing the phone. There is a file folder on the table, along with several loose pieces of paper and a pencil.)

VICTORIA. *(Into phone.)* Yes, I'd like the number for an Esther Louise Peterson at Rural Route 2 in Watson's Chapel. *(Waits.)*

GAIL. Do you really think she could still be there after thirty-five years? With the same name?

VICTORIA. *(Puts her hand over the mouthpiece.)* At least it's a place to start. *(Into phone.)* Yes. Okay, I see.

Certainly. Thank you. (*VICTORIA hangs up the phone and begins writing a note.*)

GAIL. Well?

VICTORIA. They have seven Petersons in Watson's Chapel, including an E.L. Peterson at Route 2. But the number's unlisted. (*VICTORIA finishes her note and looks up at Gail.*) It's got to be her, don't you think?

GAIL. Maybe. Now what?

VICTORIA. (*Thinks a moment.*) I'll try the post office. I'll tell them I'm sending a letter and see if they'll verify the address. (*SHE consults a piece of paper on the table for the number and begins dialing.*)

GAIL. How old would she be now? Fifty? Fifty-one?

VICTORIA. Fifty-one. God, she must have been a sophomore in high school when I was born. Can you imagine if we'd had kids when we were sophomores?

(*The LIGHTS fade on VICTORIA and GAIL and fade up on ESTHER, Victoria's birth mother, who is standing upstage right.*)

ESTHER. I was sixteen years old. For awhile, I wondered what it might be like to keep her. After all, she was *mine.* But my parents said that if I kept her, I'd be ruining my life. And theirs, too, although they never really said so. I knew that I had disappointed them.

My mother took my pregnancy very personally. She said it made her look like a terrible mother. A failure. Practically every time I looked up it seemed like she was staring at me, her eyes all wild and angry, like she just wanted a way to get me out of her house. My dad didn't get mad. But once he found out, he quit touching me. No more hugs. Just these occasional polite little pats on the shoulder. It felt like some stranger trying to get my attention so that he could ask for directions.

I was an average kid, I guess. Although in a school the size of mine, no one was really average. There were so few of us that we each had our own thing to be good at. Mine was band. I started playing the flute in the third grade and, by the time I was in junior high, I was better than all the high school flute players. Of course, there were only about five of them. But I was still better and they all hated me. I met my boyfriend, Ted, in band. He played trombone, but not very well. On my fifteenth birthday, he gave me a little silver flute on a necklace. I thought it was the most beautiful thing I'd ever seen. Ted was only the second boy I'd ever dated.

Bobby O'Halloran was the first. We actually only went out once, to a hay-rack ride with the church youth group. He held my hand.

Accidentally.

He dropped his Baby Ruth bar in the hay and was feeling around for it when he grabbed my hand by mistake. I clutched onto it for dear life and we stayed in this sort of sweaty death grip for the rest of the ride. *Very* romantic.

So, if you count Bobby, Ted was the second man in my life. Initially, we felt very grown-up to have created a child through all of our adolescent pawing and panting.

We talked about getting married; Ted was going to get a job at his father's paint store, I would finish high school, go to nursing school at St. Perpetua's over in Coldwater. We'd be the perfect young family, the pride of Watson's Chapel. The fantasies lasted about two days. Then we got frightened and angry and we broke up. We never spoke again, even when he had to sign the papers. After graduation, Ted married Betty Harrison, my next door neighbor. They had seven children. (*ESTHER laughs.*) I guess Ted never *did* figure out how birth control works.

(*LIGHTS fade out on ESTHER and up on VICTORIA and GAIL. VICTORIA is just hanging up the phone.*)

VICTORIA. Well that was almost *too* easy.
GAIL. What happened?
VICTORIA. I told the guy that I wanted to check an address and I gave him her name. He said that in a town the size of Watson's Chapel the address didn't really make a difference; if I just sent the letter it would get to her.
It looks like Esther Peterson is about to have a baby.

(*LIGHTS fade out on VICTORIA and GAIL and up on MARY. MARY is folding a child's clothing—baby and toddler clothes and putting them away in a cardboard box.)*

MARY. Andrew and I planned to have exactly four children. I have no idea how we arrived at that number, but for some reason we thought it was ideal. We had names picked out before we even got engaged. We agreed that we each got to pick two names, one of each sex. I picked Andrew, Jr. and Victoria. Andrew picked William and—Augusta, after his Swedish grandmother. Maybe it's fortunate that we just had the one girl.
We wanted to wait a year or two, so that Andrew could get his insurance business established. When we got married, Fr. Basil gave us a magnetic St. Christopher for

the car and a little booklet about the rhythm method. So we tried it. My sister, Martha, said, "You know what they call a woman who uses rhythm, don't you? Mommy."

Well, everyone was amazed when it worked for us for the first year, then the second and third. What they didn't know was that we had been trying to have a child for most of that time.

When I finally did get pregnant, we were ecstatic. We went out to dinner to celebrate. We had prime rib and even ordered big shrimp cocktails beforehand. Spent most of our grocery money and had to eat boxed macaroni and cheese for a week. But three weeks later I miscarried. I got pregnant two more times; by the third time we didn't bother to celebrate. We just waited for what we knew was coming. It was worse that time the cramps, the bleeding. And as that little life was drained out of me, I felt as if mine went along with it.

(MARY turns toward Esther as her LIGHT fades out and the LIGHTS in Esther's area come up.)

ESTHER. It's strange, you always read about girls going to other cities, or finding another doctor to do their pregnancy test. It's all very secret, very discreet. (*SHE laughs.*) Well, not for me it wasn't.

I thought I had the flu—nausea, fatigue. It sure never occurred to me that I might be pregnant. That happened to other girls. Girls that people made fun of. Like Kathy Jo Sippel. She got pregnant when she was a junior. Everybody said she didn't even know who the father was. The big joke was that they were taking bets to see if the football team or the wrestling team got named as the father. Kathy Jo got sent away to live with some mysterious "aunt" in Cleveland and before long we forgot all about her. I never thought the way they talked about her seemed very nice, but at the time I guess I thought she deserved it. I mean, she did get caught playing strip poker with the American Legion color guard after the Fourth of July parade. At least, that's what my brother, Matthew, told me. Kathy Jo was pretty wild. And I was nothing like her.

My mom figured it out before I did. She marched me down to Dr. Pinkerton's office and demanded that he do a pregnancy test. I thought she was crazy! A pregnancy test? But she insisted. She even stayed in the room while he examined me. I was mortified. Not only was it my first pelvic exam, but I had my mother there glaring at me during the whole thing like somebody waiting while a mechanic checks under the hood of an undependable car.

Welcome to womanhood, Esther.

Before long the whole town knew. Aside from a couple of my friends and my brother, no one ever asked me how I felt or what my plans were or even if I was scared. There I was swelling up right in front of them and it was like no one noticed. Or wanted to notice.

(LIGHTS fade on ESTHER and come up on VICTORIA and GAIL. THEY are studying a map. Gail is eating a doughnut.)

GAIL. *(Pointing.)* Is that it? It's bigger than I expected.
VICTORIA. *(Looks closely, then scrapes at the map with her thumbnail.)* That's icing from your doughnut. Here's Watson's Chapel. Right here.

GAIL. It sure is small. What's the population?

VICTORIA. *(Consulting the back of the map.)* Let's see. Eight hundred and thirty-nine. And this map is a couple of years old, so if anything it's probably smaller than that by now.

GAIL. Jesus. They must have all known about you. I'll bet you were the talk of the town. Well, this will be easy. Just go into town, stop at the first feed store or the Cozy Cafe or whatever and say, "Hi, I'm the little Peterson kid who caused such a stir back in 'fifty-five. Now, point me toward Edna Lucille."

VICTORIA. *(Laughing.)* It's Esther Louise and somehow I'd pictured being a little more subtle about it. *(VICTORIA begins to fold up the map.)*

GAIL. Look, Vic. I wish you'd reconsider about telling your mom. She should hear this from you and not from someone else.

VICTORIA. *(Accusingly.)* Who else could she possibly hear it from?

GAIL. Mothers have that weird sixth sense. Like the way your mom always knew when we'd sneak the leftover wine from Thanksgiving dinner up to your room.

VICTORIA. We? That was always *your* idea.

GAIL. It was *never* my idea. It was yours. It was my idea to put the Chablis in the empty Listerine bottle. She'll never forgive us for letting her gargle with Gallo.

(THEY both laugh.)

GAIL. Vic, it's been twenty-three years since you found out. Maybe it's time to put this to rest.

VICTORIA. That's what I trying to do, Gail. That's exactly what I am trying to do.

(LIGHTS fade out on GAIL as VICTORIA crosses downstage.)

VICTORIA. When I first found out, I didn't tell anyone. Not even Gail and we usually told each other everything.

For a month or so I would go to my parents' room every time they were gone and get those papers out and look at them again. I would think of excuses to stay home. I'd tell them that I needed to work on a book report for English or that I wanted to rearrange the sweaters in my closet. As soon as my dad's old Chevrolet turned the corner, I would race up the stairs. Each time I opened the drawer, I thought that the folder would be gone and that would mean that it really wasn't true. But it was always there.

I read those papers until I knew every word. The judge's name Edwin D. Hughes, Jr.—the lawyers' names, even the number of the State of Ohio form that the thing was printed on. I read them over and over. Then I put them back in the drawer. I was really careful to put back all my dad's socks just like he had them. Lined up in soft little bundles. Blue, black, brown. With the orange and green argyle ones that I had given him for Father's Day tucked way in the back. No one knew.

I waited for just the right moment.

(LIGHTS fade up on MARY.)

VICTORIA. I still remember what it was about. (*VICTORIA, now thirteen, turns to face Mary.*) But, Mom. It's the grand opening of the roller rink. There are prizes and contests and everything. I just know I can win that race where you have to skate backwards. I've been practicing in the driveway for two weeks.

(*MARY shakes her head.*)

VICTORIA. Come on, Mom. Everybody else is going to be there. The Zeroni twins went at noon just to be the first ones in the door. Gail is going and she can't even skate. I'll be the only one who isn't there. It's not fair.

MARY. Victoria, I'm sorry that you think I'm being unfair but we've been over this before. You can't stay out past nine on a school night. You have your homework—isn't your science report due next week? And you need to be in bed by ten. (*MARY puts her arm around Victoria.*) You're a growing girl, you need to get your sleep.

VICTORIA. (*Pulls away.*) I'll bet my *real* mother would let me go. She'd never treat me like this.

(*MARY looks horrified, but not necessarily surprised. SHE opens her mouth, but no sound comes out. The TWO face each other for awhile, then MARY turns and exits quickly. The LIGHTS in Mary's area fade out.*)

VICTORIA. She didn't come out again until the next day. My father made excuses for her, said she didn't feel well. We both knew he was lying. He made tomato soup and grilled cheese sandwiches for dinner. Then he suggested that we all turn in early; it was seven o'clock. He went to their room and closed the door behind him.

It was a long time until they left me home alone again. Finally, one Saturday morning they went across town to Foster's Greenhouse to pick out the plants for my mother's flower boxes. She always planted the same thing—red and white petunias. The fancy kind with the ruffled edges. I told them that I didn't want to go along; that I was staying home to polish my shoes for Mass the next day. I watched the car turn and even waited a few minutes just to make sure that it wasn't some kind of trick. (*After a moment, VICTORIA turns and walks slowly up the steps to Mary's area.*) I wanted to run, to take the stairs two at a time. But I made myself walk. Of course, when I looked, the papers were gone. I checked the other drawers, the shelves in their closet. I went crazy. Looking under the mattress, in my mother's cedar hope chest. I looked in shoeboxes, between the pages of books, behind the smiling family picture in the fancy gold frame. Nothing. All that remained of my former life. Hidden once again.

(MARY enters. VICTORIA does not turn to face her.)

VICTORIA. So you thought you were doing the right thing by not telling me to begin with. Right?

MARY. Yes, Vickie. We believed they knew what was best. Even Fr. Basil said ...

VICTORIA. Okay, okay. But once I'd found the papers, once I knew ... (*SHE turns to face Mary.*) Why did you hide them again?

MARY. We took them to the bank and put them in a safety deposit box. We'd been meaning to for a long time...

VICTORIA. And Little Orphan Annie's discovery gave you just the motivation that you needed.

MARY. *(Angry.)* You're not an orphan, Victoria. You are my daughter. You have been from the moment they first put you in my arms. We made a stupid mistake in not telling you; but that doesn't make me any less your mother.

(Mary's LIGHTS fade as VICTORIA crosses down out of Mary's area and back into her own. LIGHTS come up center. GAIL is still seated at the table. SHE is holding the bird and trying to get it to drink from an eyedropper.)

VICTORIA. Gail, I'm not some kid who believes that her real mother is a ballerina or an astronaut or something. I don't want to make my mother miserable and I'm not out to hurt this Esther person either. It's just that there has always been this part of me that I have never known about. Even before I knew I was adopted I could sense something. Like part of me was missing. Or like I'd lived another life that I just couldn't quite remember. I *have* to know about her. I have had so many pictures in my head; I just want to know what the real picture looks like. Can't you understand that?

GAIL. *(Puts the bird back in its box and stands)* Look, I love you and your mom and I don't want to see either of you disappointed or hurt. But I suppose if I were you I'd have to know too. I hope it works out for you, Vic.

Really. (*GAIL hugs Victoria.*) Hey, you'd better get on the road.

(*VICTORIA exits briefly as GAIL continues to feed the bird. VICTORIA re-enters carrying a suitcase, a large photo album, and a shoebox.*)

VICTORIA. Well, I guess I'm all set. I thought I'd take along a photo album.

GAIL. Good idea. Thirty-five years at a glance. What's in it?

VICTORIA. (*Opens the photo album and sits next to Gail.*) This is my first birthday.

GAIL. Is that me? That bald kid?

VICTORIA. With both hands in the cake. Yes, it is. Things haven't changed much have they?

GAIL. (*Laughing.*) No, not really.

VICTORIA. (*Turns page.*) This is my first piano recital. I left out the pictures of my next two hundred piano recitals. God, I looked like quite the priss, didn't I?

GAIL. You always wore those frilly yellow dresses and big poofy hair bows. And your shoes were always dyed to match. You looked like an Easter basket. It was disgusting.

VICTORIA. (*Laughing.*) So I guess it's fair to say that you weren't my biggest fan.

GAIL. I really hated your recitals. It always seemed like they were on the first nice day of spring. I wanted to be outside, not all dressed up listening to twenty kids play the same song. (*SHE hums a little of "Fur Elise."*) Then all the way home Mom would tell me how talented you were and how she wished I could find something that I was good at too.

VICTORIA. Gail, I'm sorry. I didn't realize ...

GAIL. Oh, it's okay. I hated going until that one what were you? nine? ten?— when you threw up all over your piano teacher. That made it all worthwhile for me.

VICTORIA. I was ten. Mrs. Rozenboom never quite forgave me. *(Laughs.)* She always sat really far away from me during my lessons after that.

GAIL. *(Pointing to shoebox.)* What's that? Taking her your baby shoes or did you get her a pair of high tops for Mother's Day?

VICTORIA. It's probably kind of dumb, but ever since I was fourteen I've gotten my mom—my other mom—a Mother's Day card. When I'd pick out one for Mom—Mary—I'd get one just like it for my birth mother. Pretty corny, isn't it?

GAIL. No, it's nice. Really. I bet she'll appreciate it. If you find her.

VICTORIA. I'll find her. I really feel like this is supposed to work out.

GAIL. Vic, what if she doesn't want to see you? I mean, shouldn't she have some choice in this.

VICTORIA. She didn't give me much of a choice when I was a baby. She made a decision for me and now I'm making one for her.

I'm not naive about this. I know it will be a shock to her. Can you imagine what it would be like to see your daughter after thirty-five years? I wonder if she even saw me when I was born. *(Pause.)* Well, I'd better take off; it's a long drive. You sure you'll be okay with Mr. Welter?

GAIL. I'm sure. I'm thinking of enrolling him in obedience school while you're gone. Maybe teach him to do some chores and things around the house. Just call and let me know what's going on, okay? I can still go along if you want.

VICTORIA. No, I'll be fine. I promise I'll call as soon as I know something. (*VICTORIA begins to get her photo album and box of cards ready.*) Look, Gail, a few days ago you tried to talk me out of this. Why are you so supportive all of a sudden? I appreciate it; I just don't understand it.

GAIL. Ever since junior high—when you found out about being adopted—you've been distant, withdrawn.

VICTORIA. Since when have I been distant from you?

GAIL. Not with me. But when other people get too close, you start to panic.

Like Jerry. He was a great guy, funny, smart. Smelled good. But once it looked like you two were headed toward something a little more significant than a friendship, you dumped him.

Even the animals; you just have these strays that you bring home. Baby squirrels, bunnies with broken legs, birds who fell out of the nest. You keep them for awhile and then let them go. You really love animals but you've never had a dog or a cat or even a bowl of goldfish. Only wild animals that you know will be leaving.

God, look at your job, Vic. You're a great photographer. Really talented. But you always take photographs of mountains or trees or beaches. Things that can't disappoint you.

You want to find out where you came from; *I'd* like to see where you could go. (*Pause.*) Now, on to important matters.

I put some essentials in the car for you. Oreos, a pound of malted milk balls, some Granny Smiths, and about ten different flavors of gum. And I picked up a copy of *The*

Mayor of Casterbridge on cassette to help you pass the time.

VICTORIA. Thanks, but why Thomas Hardy?

GAIL. They didn't have much left at the library. And since this lasts eleven hours and twenty-seven minutes, you'll be able to drive to Ohio and back several times before you finish it. (*GAIL picks up the bird box.*) Come on. Mr. Welter wants to walk you to the car.

(*GAIL and VICTORIA exit. LIGHTS come up on ESTHER. SHE is holding a small pink teddy bear wrapped in a blanket.*)

ESTHER. In the hospital, they told me that I couldn't see her. Didn't even ask if I wanted to. Mrs. Ryan, my social worker, told me it would be better that way. Better for who, Mrs. Ryan?

MRS. RYAN. She'll have the chance for a real home now. You'll forget in time, dear. Go back to your life and put this all behind you, just like a bad dream.

ESTHER. You go to hell, Mrs. Ryan.

One of the nurses on the night shift, Phyllis, was really nice to me. She was the only one there who seemed to really understand what I was feeling. On my second night in the hospital, Phyllis woke me up. It was a Saturday; it must have been one or two in the morning and the hospital was dark and quiet for once. We walked past the other nurse, who was asleep with her head on the desk. She had a little portable radio next to her but there wasn't any music. Just static. Phyllis led me into the nursery. There were all these babies lined up, wrapped in pink or blue blankets.

My baby wasn't with the others. She was in a room in the back all by herself. Only two days old and already an outcast. I sat in an old rocker that had been painted white and had decals of little smiling sheep on it.

(ESTHER sits in the rocker holding the bear. SHE gently unwraps the blanket and in turn kisses each foot, each hand, and the bear's nose. SHE stares at the "baby" for a long time, memorizing its face, before she speaks again.)

We had one hour together. One hour that has had to last for thirty-five years.

(LIGHTS fade out on ESTHER and up on MARY. SHE is holding a teddy bear. It is old and beat-up looking. It has obviously seen much love.)

MARY. It was a Tuesday. Tuesday, May first. Mrs. Ryan called at about nine in the morning. "We have a baby for you, Mary. A little girl." A baby? (*SHE laughs.*) We got to the agency and they took us to a little room that had an old plaid couch and a painting of ducks and geese on the wall. It seemed like we waited there forever. I counted all the ducks in the painting, then all the geese, and was just starting in on the cattails when Mrs. Ryan came in carrying the littlest bundle of child I had ever seen. She handed her to me and said, "Here's your daughter." Then she left us alone. Our first time as a family. We didn't know what to do exactly; we were almost afraid to touch her. We uncovered her arms and she grabbed onto one of

Andrew's fingers. He immediately turned to mush and stayed that way with her his entire life.

The pictures we have from that day are funny. We took turns taking each other's picture with the baby. It's hard to tell which of us looks more awkward with her. Andrew is holding her way out in front of him, like he's afraid he'll crush her if she gets too close. And I have my arm cocked with my elbow way up in the air as if I think she has to stay perpendicular. (*SHE demonstrates with the bear.*) We really didn't know what we were doing. My great aunt, Frieda, had warned us to be careful when we gave Victoria her bath. "She's got no muscle control, you know. Hang onto her head so it doesn't bounce around or she'll get brain damage." We were terrified. That night, for her first bath, Andrew got out the baby book, turned to the chapter on bathing and read each step out loud to me while I followed his instructions. He held the book in his right hand and with his left he held Victoria's head like a ripe honeydew. (*Laughs.*) I have had a good life; some wonderful things have happened to me. But nothing has ever compared with the elation and the joy and the love that I felt on the day we brought our daughter home.

(*LIGHTS fade out on MARY and up on VICTORIA, downstage left, and GAIL, downstage right. THEY are talking on the telephone.*)

VICTORIA. Gail, I've found her.
GAIL. What's she like? What did she say? God, that didn't take long at all.
VICTORIA. I haven't talked to her yet.
GAIL. How did you find her?

VICTORIA. Voter registration records. The woman at the courthouse said she was ...

GAIL. Republican or Democrat?

VICTORIA. I don't know.

GAIL. You don't *know*?

VICTORIA. I didn't ask. I don't think they can tell you. Anyway, they gave me her address—and her phone number.

GAIL. I thought it was unlisted.

VICTORIA. Evidently she didn't tell them that when she registered to vote. They didn't blink an eye when they gave it to me. I tried to act very calm, like it didn't matter, but I was practically peeing in my pants.

GAIL. *(Laughs.)* What's your next move?

VICTORIA. I'm going to call her—just as soon as I figure out what to say.

GAIL. Vic, your mom called. She was hoping you'd be able to come home to help her get the garden in.

VICTORIA. I'll call her in a day or so. How's Mr. Welter doing?

GAIL. He's great, getting stronger every day. He's developed quite an appetite; I spent two hours yesterday hunting for bugs on my bushes. Then he wouldn't eat any of the bugs. I was going to look for worms, I figured he's big enough to try them now. But I couldn't find any in my yard or yours, so I ended up spending four dollars in one of those vend-a-bait machines at the Come 'n' Go. He thought they were delectable, even asked for my recipe. Hey, let me know what happens, Vic, and good luck.

(LIGHTS fade on GAIL. VICTORIA crosses to center as LIGHTS come up on MARY.)

MARY. My niece, Gail, is possibly the worst liar in the world. When I called, she gave me a well-rehearsed speech about Vickie being gone for a few days. *(SHE pretends that she is reading from a sheet of paper.)* "She-had-the-chance-to-stay-at-a-friend's-house-on-Willow-Lake-and-thought-she-could-get-some-good-spring-photography-done." *(Laughs.)* No, as soon as Gail answered the phone, I knew something was up. And I had a pretty good idea what it was.

I saw that magazine in Vickie's house when I visited there last. It fell open to the page on Ohio, as though she had read it over and over. And I learned what my daughter already knew. Her records are open. I knew she'd follow up on it and, in a way, I guess that I hoped she would.

(LIGHTS fade on MARY. LIGHTS come up on VICTORIA and begin to fade up slowly on ESTHER during Victoria's lines.)

VICTORIA. I must have driven by her house twenty times, each time searching it for another detail. It was only about a mile out of town, on a gravel road. It was a two-story. Painted brick red with white trim and shutters. The paint looked fresh and the yard was so neat it looked as though it had been vacuumed. There was a huge red maple in the front yard with an old tire swing hanging from it. Did I have brothers and sisters who used to play there? Why did they get to stay with her and I had to leave? What was wrong with me that I was given away?

Gail was right, of course. I don't let other people see into me. I shut them out before they have a chance to hurt me. I try not to need them. Just like this Esther didn't need me.

But I knew that I needed to hear the story from her, so I stopped the car at a telephone booth. I practiced my speech over and over and finally I worked up the nerve to call her.

Hello. Is this Esther Peterson? Esther Louise Peterson?

My name is Victoria Drake. I've been thinking about this for a long time and I felt that I needed to call you. My birthday is April 27th; I'm your daughter and I would really like to talk with you.

(ESTHER begins smoothing her clothes and hair and straightening her furniture.)

ESTHER. You see things like this on television all the time. And I suppose that I'd always fantasized about what it might be like if she called me. But I never really believed that she would. It never occurred to me that it might be a prank or a wrong number. I knew it was real. I gave her my address and then spent the next few minutes in a panic. What should I wear? Did the house look nice enough?

(VICTORIA climbs the steps to Esther's platform. SHE is carrying the box of cards and the photo album.
ESTHER goes to meet Victoria. THEY face one another as the LIGHTS fade out on them and up on MARY.)

MARY. When people ask me how I'd feel if Victoria wanted to find her birth mother, I always try to sound as if my main concern is how the other mother might feel. I go on about how she should have some right to privacy. What if she doesn't want to be found, I ask them. And I do believe that all of that is important. But deep inside, I've been terrified.

But, really, Mary. What do you have to be afraid of? Victoria is your daughter. She knows that you've always been here for her. What could this woman possibly have to offer that you don't? (*Laughs, starts to exit, then stops.*) She probably knows how to knit. I'll be she makes all of her own clothes. Probably teaches classes in knitting. Or wrote a book on it. I never could knit. Or sew either.

I imagine she's a lot younger than I am. She probably knows how to drive a stick shift and has seen all the movies that get nominated for Oscars. She and Victoria will get to be great friends, they'll go on trips to Cancun together and then compare tans. They'll be in one of those detergent ads where the mother and daughter's hands look just alike. (*MARY stops, realized what she has been saying, and laughs.*) "Well, now, Mar. You're getting a little out of control. Time for a reality pill." That's what Andrew would say to me right now. (*MARY sits.*) Oh Andrew. I've lost *you*. Isn't that enough?

(Mary's LIGHTS fade slightly. LIGHTS up on VICTORIA and ESTHER, who are now seated. BOTH look slightly uncomfortable. VICTORIA is still clutching the box of cards.)

VICTORIA. Did you ever get married?
ESTHER. Oh, yes. Once. Several years after you were born. He was an intern at the hospital where I was working. He kept putting me off about starting a family, said he wanted to wait until he started practicing on his own. One afternoon I sprained an ankle at work, tripped

over some patient's wheelchair. My foot swelled up as big as a telephone pole, so I went home early. I found him there with one of his former patients. Seemed he'd already been practicing with her for quite some time.

VICTORIA. What a shit.

ESTHER. *(Laughing.)* Exactly. So that's when I moved back to Watson's Chapel. They needed a head nurse at the Catholic hospital over in Coldwater and it just felt right to come live here at my grandmother's old house. I was always so at home here. I even left that tire swing in the maple tree. We all had such fun with it when we were kids.

My parents moved into a condo in Cincinnati—to be close to my brother and his family. He was one of their "good" children, you see. With them gone, it seemed safe for me to move back here. Besides, I was tired of being the person that everybody else felt I should be. I wanted to come back home and just be the Esther that *I* wanted to be. So, I play my flute in my nightgown, I drive a red pick-up, and I sometimes eat an entire pint of chocolate chip ice cream right out of the container.

Enough stories about me for now. Tell me about your parents.

VICTORIA. It sounds odd. Hearing you call them my parents.

ESTHER. Victoria, I gave birth to you. Then I let you go. They were the ones who were there for the chicken pox and the skinned elbows and the temper tantrums. *(Smiles sadly.)* And your first steps and the piano recitals and your senior prom. So, go ahead. Tell me about them.

VICTORIA. I don't know where to start. My dad is dead. He had a heart attack three years ago. No warning or anything. Just died. The thing I remember best about him is how easy-going he was. Never complained, rarely criticized. And when he did, it was really good-natured. Whenever I'd get cranky he'd say, "Vickie, you're turning into the grumpasaurus again." Then I'd laugh and forget what I'd been crabby about. It always worked—even after I was grownup.

And he was willing to try anything. Since I didn't have brothers and sisters, he used to go sledding and skating and all those things with me. He even broke his wrist once going down one of those giant slides at the state fair.

ESTHER. Sounds like a nice man. And a good sport.

VICTORIA. *(Smiling.)* Yes, I guess he was. He was a real good sport.

ESTHER. What about your mom? Was she good to you?

VICTORIA. My mom. Yes, she was good to me. Looking back, there are some things I wish she had done differently, but I think maybe she did the best she could.

ESTHER. Don't be too hard on her, Victoria; it couldn't have been easy for her. I assume they couldn't have children?

VICTORIA. Right. I'm not sure what the reason was. I know she had a lot of miscarriages and they warned her about getting pregnant.

ESTHER. Victoria, women my age grew up being told what to do, how to look, what to wear, who to marry. And the main thing that we were told was that our purpose for being here was to become a mother. I did the right things, I just got the order confused.

Your mom is older than I am so it must have been even worse for her. All that be fruitful and multiply stuff. I mean, what does that say about you if you *can't* multiply?

I had no idea what I was doing when I had you. My parents and this lady from the agency all told me what to do. I'd like to be able to tell you that I had some great humanitarian reason for giving you up. Some wise cosmic plan for your life. The truth is I was just trying to do whatever I had to do to be everybody's good girl again. I had disappointed them all—they made sure I knew that. It's bad enough to disappoint someone you love. You don't need to have them remind you of it.

(LIGHTS fade slightly on ESTHER and VICTORIA and come up on MARY, who is sorting through a shoebox of mass cards.)

MARY. I know what she gave to us. This mother of my child has always been in my thoughts. Every year, on Victoria's birthday, I have had the priest say two masses. One for Vickie and one for the woman who gave her life. I have always tried to do what was best. For both of them. (*MARY holds up one of the cards.*) This is from her seventh birthday. She had to have her tonsils out the day before and the nurses gave her a surprise party.

(LIGHTS remain up on MARY as they come up on VICTORIA and ESTHER. THEY are looking at the Mother's Day cards. ESTHER is looking at a particularly large card.)

VICTORIA. That was when I was fourteen. My dad gave me five dollars because I did so well on my report card and I spent it all on the biggest cards I could find. Smell it.

I squirted them with White Shoulders perfume from the tester bottle at Maxwell's Pharmacy.

MARY. Thirteen. The year she found the papers.

VICTORIA. Fifteen. We had to draw a family tree in our English class. I drew a trunk with no branches or leaves and said I didn't know what my tree looked like. I got an F.

MARY. Andrew always said, "Mary, we are her parents. Nothing can change that. Her home is with us and she'll always come back again." I really want to believe that now.

(LIGHTS fade out on MARY. ESTHER and VICTORIA move toward the stairs; VICTORIA is preparing to leave.)

VICTORIA. I feel like we have a lot more to talk about. I'd like to stay in touch, if that's all right.

ESTHER. Yes, of course it is. *(Pause.)* Victoria? I am so sorry. You understand, don't you? Letting you go was the hardest thing I've ever done in my life. It was also one of the smartest things. Look at all that you've done and seen that wouldn't have been possible with a sixteen-year old kid for a mother.

VICTORIA. I understand, Esther. At least I'm trying to.

I didn't before. I was angry with you. I felt like you'd abandoned me, that I wasn't the daughter you wanted. In a way, I think I came here hoping that I wouldn't like you. That I could do something to make you hurt the way I have.

But now, I'm glad that I found you.

ESTHER. Me, too. More than you'll ever know. I want you to have this. It was my grandmother's. (*SHE gives VICTORIA a necklace with a locket and helps her put it on.*) You would have liked Grandma Rosie. She always referred to my mother as "Rosemary's Baby." It made my mother furious. "Demonic possession is no laughing matter" she'd say, which always made Grandma laugh even harder. Grandma Rosie was one of the few people in my family I felt like I actually might be related to. The next time you're here, I'll dig out some pictures of her.

And Victoria, don't be so hard on your mom. We all just did what we were told.

(*VICTORIA and ESTHER have an awkward moment in which THEY are uncertain if they should shake hands or embrace. Finally, THEY hug one another tentatively and VICTORIA crosses back down the stairs. The LIGHTS fade on ESTHER. VICTORIA and GAIL cross to their earlier "telephone" places.*)

GAIL. So do you look like her?
VICTORIA. No, not really. She did say that I have a Peterson nose. But I saw pictures of the other Petersons so I'm not sure if that's a compliment or not.

And get this! My father is some guy named Theodore Trimble. He owns a paint store in Chalkville. Ted's World O'Color. Can you believe that? It's about ten miles from here, but I don't think I'll look him up on this trip. Meeting Esther was enough.

GAIL. Do you have a lot in common?
VICTORIA. Not a lot. We both have hay fever and neither of us likes country music. I wish I would have

gotten her cooking skills. She fixed some great fried chicken with mashed potatoes. And some sort of vegetable casserole with carrots and beans and brussels sprouts.

GAIL. Are you disappointed?

VICTORIA. No, I ate around them.

GAIL. Not about the sprouts. About meeting Esther.

VICTORIA. Maybe. In a way, I guess I'd expected something different. More answers or something.

GAIL. When are you starting back? There's a thirty-pound robin here who misses you.

VICTORIA. I'm thinking of taking a couple more days. There's something else I need to do. If you think Mr. Welter looks strong enough, go ahead and let him go.

GAIL. You don't want to be here for that?

VICTORIA. No, go ahead. You've spent all this time with him, buying him worms and everything. You should be the one who's there for his first solo flight.

(LIGHTS fade out on GAIL and up on MARY. SHE is dressed in work clothes and is raking. A second rake leans against the wall. VICTORIA crosses to Mary's platform. MARY looks up and SHE and VICTORIA look at one another for a long time before Victoria speaks.)

VICTORIA. You're not planning to plant brussels sprouts there are you?

MARY. No. I'd never plant brussels sprouts. My daughter hates them.

(THEY continue to look at one another. Finally, VICTORIA picks up the other rake and begins raking. MARY watches, smiles, and goes back to work as LIGHTS fade.)

PROPERTY PLOT

Bird
Small cardboard box
Towel
Mixing bowl
Spoon
Birdseed
Hard-boiled egg
Raisins
Envelope with birth certificate
File folder and papers
Pencil
Cardboard box with baby clothes
Map
Doughnut
Eyedropper
Suitcase
Photo album
Shoebox with Mother's Day cards
Small teddy bear wrapped in a blanket
Shoebox with mass cards
Teddy bear
Necklace with locket
Rakes (2)

Other Publications For Your Interest

SIS BOOM BAA. Comedy. Sybil Rosen. 2m., 4f. Int. Football widows of America: This Is Your Life! Pam, Cheryl, Linda and Mary are best friends. They do everything together—because their husbands spend most of their time watching football on TV. Says Pam: "Compulsive football-watching is a male-reaction formation to the stress of being civilized. It's more bonding than Crazy Glue." Mary, the new-comer to the group has recently married Joey, and his obsession is really getting to her. While the women cook New Year's Day dinner in Cheryl's kitchen they coach Mary on technique—on how to get Joey's attention away from the game. We finally meet Joey when he comes into the kitchen for something to eat; and Mary tries what she has learned on him, to no avail—so she tackles him! **(#21681)**

FREEZE TAG. Comedy. Jacquelyn Reingold. 2f Ext. When Andrea tries to buy a newspaper in NYC's East Village, she is thrust onto an emotional journey she will never forget. Aldrich, the newsstand vendor, seems to know the most intimate secrets of Andrea's life, from childhood up to the present moment, including who her boyfriend is sleeping with and why. In this funny and touching play, two women are forced to confront who they are, who they once were, and what it means to be a friend. "Gripping and hilarious."—N.Y. Times. "Really terrific . . . one of the most impressive [playwriting] debuts of the season."—N.Y. Press. "An extraordinary play . . . an unforgettable experience."—Back Stage. **(#8678)**

LOOKIN' FOR A BETTER BERRY BUSH. Comic Drama. Jean Lenox Toddie (author of *Tell Me Another Story Sing Me a Song, A Scent of Honeysuckle* and *A Bag of Green Apples*). 2f. Ext. (simply suggested). Emma and Addie confront each other on the sidewalk of a city neighborhood. Emma is a proper woman who worked in a diner for forty years and "served more cups of coffee than you can count if you live to be a hundred." Addie, a street woman whose papa "set us t' wanderin' jes' a-lookin' fer a better berry bush," rummages in trash cans and sleeps in a cardboard box. This is the humorous and touching tale of two women, alienated from each other by vastly different life experience, who clash on a city street, only to find themselves sitting down together on a stoop in front of a brownstone, and tentatively reaching out for mutual understanding. **(#14927)**

TONE CLUSTERS

Joyce Carol Oates

Drama

1m., 1f., plus 1 male voice. Bare stage. Frank and Emily Gulick are a nice middle-American couple with a nice house in a nice neighborhood. Why, then are they obviously under so much strain? As they are interviewed by an unseen interrogator, their story, and their predicament, emerges. The mutilated body of a 14 year-old girl from the neighborhood has been found in their basement, and their son is charged with the murder. Desperately, they cling to the belief that their son is not guilty, even as it becomes increasingly clear that he is the murderer. And, even as we are moved by the pitiable Gulicks, we ask ourselves, do they somehow share in the guilt of the crime? And: could we, as parents, someday find ourselves in their predicament? This extraordinary play by one of America's foremost women of letters won the prestigious Heideman Award bestowed by Actors Theatre of Louisville, which commissioned it and gave it its world premier at the famed Humana Festival. In *In Darkest America*.   (#22727)

THE ECLIPSE

Joyce Carol Oates

Drama

1m., 3f Int. Stephanie Washburn, a middle-aged college professor, lives with her mother Muriel in a small apartment in Philadelphia. Muriel was once a brilliant high school teacher. Now, she is retired, and her mind is going, possibly from Alzheimer's disease. As she goes in and out of reality, she makes her daughter's life miserable, even going so far as to call the local department of social services to accuse Stephanie of abusing her—a total fabrication, of course. Muriel also has a fantasy that she has a Latin lover, a Señor Rios, with whom she is carrying on a torrid affair. There is no Señor Rios, of course. Or is there? In the end, as flamenco music plays, Muriel enters, in a Spanish dancing dress, for her big date with Señor Rios, who appears, exactly as Muriel has described him, for a torrid dance with Muriel around the apartment as Stephanie sleeps in a chair, oblivious to it all. Then Muriel leaves for her date with the dark gentleman, and both women are finally released from their suffering. Death has finally claimed Muriel. This haunting play by one of America's foremost women of letters was commissioned by the Actors Theatre of Louisville, which produced it as part of their famed Humana Festival, and was subsequently produced Off Broadway in New York by Ensemble Studio Theatre. In *In Darkest America*.   (#7633)

RAVENSCROFT. (Little Theatre.) Mystery. Don Nigro. 1m., 5f. Simple unit set. This unusual play is several cuts above the genre it explores, a Gothic thriller for groups that don't usually do such things, a thinking person's mystery, a dark comedy that is at times immensely funny and at others quite frightening. On a snowy night, Inspector Ruffing is called to a remote English country house to investigate the headlong plunge of a young manservant, Patrick Roarke, down the main staircase, and finds himself getting increasingly involved in the lives of five alluring and dangerous women— Marcy, the beautiful Viennese governess with a past, Mrs. Ravenscroft, the flirtatious and chattery lady of the manor, Gillian, her charming but possibly demented daughter, Mrs. French, the formidable and passionate cook, and Dolly, a frantic and terrified little maid—who lead him through an increasingly bewildering labyrinth of contradictory versions of what happened to Patrick and to the dead Mr. Ravenscroft before him. There are ghosts at the top of the staircase, skeletons in the closet, and much more than the Inspector had bargained for as his quest to solve one mystery leads him deeper and deeper into others and to an investigation of his own tortured soul and the nature of truth itself. You will not guess the ending, but you will be teased, seduced, bewildered, amused, frightened and led along with the Inspector to a dark encounter with truth, or something even stranger. A funny, first rate psychological mystery, and more.

(#19987)

DARK SONNETS OF THE LADY, THE. (Advanced Groups.) Drama. Don Nigro. 4m., 4f. Unit set. First produced professionally at the McCarter Theatre in Princeton and a finalist for the National Play Award, this stunningly theatrical and very funny drama takes place in Vienna in the fall of the year 1900, when Dora, a beautiful and brilliant young girl, walks into the office of Sigmund Freud, then an obscure doctor in his forties, to begin the most famous and controversial encounter in the history of psychoanalysis. Dora is funny, suspicious, sarcastic and elusive, and Freud become fascinated and obsessed by her and by the intricate labyrinth of her illness. He moves like a detective through the mystery of her life, and we meet in the course of his journey through her mind: her lecherous father, her obsessively house-cleaning mother, her irritating brother, her sinister admirer Herr Klippstein and his sensual and seductive wife, and their pretty and lost little governess. Nightmares, fantasies, hallucinations and memories all come alive onstage in a wild kaleidoscopic tapestry as Freud moves closer and closer to the truth about Dora's murky past, and the play becomes a kind of war between the two of them about what the truth is, about the uneasy truce between men and women, and ultimately a tragic love story. Laced throughout with eerie and haunting Strauss waltzes, this is a rich, complex, challenging and delightfully intriguing universe, a series of riddles one inside the other that lead the audience step by step to the center of Dora's troubled soul and her innermost secrets. Is Dora sick, or is the corrupt patriarchal society in which she and Freud are both trapped the real source of a complex group neurosis that binds all the characters together in a dark web of desperate erotic relationships, a kind of beautiful, insane and terrible dance of life, desire and death?

(#5952)

NEW COMEDIES FROM
SAMUEL FRENCH, INC.

MAIDS OF HONOR. (Little Theatre.) Comedy. Joan Casademont. 3m., 4f. Comb Int./Ext. Elizabeth McGovern, Laila Robins and Kyra Sedgwick starred in this warm, wacky comedy at Off-Broadway's famed WPA Theatre. Monica Bowlin, a local TV talk-show host, is getting married. Her two sisters, Isabelle and Annie, are intent on talking her out of it. It seems that Mr. Wonderful, the groom-to-be, is about to be indicted for insider trading, a little secret he has failed to share with his fiancee, Monica. She has a secret she has kept herself, too—she's pregnant, possibly not by her groom-to-be! All this is uncovered by delightfully kookie Isabelle, who aspires to be an investigative reporter. She'd also like to get Monica to realize that she is marrying the wrong man, for the wrong reason. She should be marrying ex-boyfriend Roger Dowling, who has come back to return a diary Monica left behind. And sister Annie should be marrying the caterer for the wedding, old flame Harry Hobson—but for some reason she can't relax enough to see how perfect he is for her. The reason for all three Bowlin women's difficulties with men, the reason why they have always made the wrong choice and failed to see the right one, is that they are the adult children of an alcoholic father and an abused mother, both now passed away, and they cannot allow themselves to love because they themselves feel unlovable. Sound gloomy and depressing? No, indeed. This delightful, wise and warm-hearted new play is loaded with laughs. We would also like to point out to all you actors that the play is also loaded with excellent monologues, at least one of which was recently included in an anthology of monologues from the best new plays.)   (#14961)

GROTESQUE LOVESONGS. (Little Theatre.) Comedy. Don Nigro. (Author of *The Curate Shakespeare As You Like It, Seascape with Sharks and Dancer* and other plays). This quirky new comedy about a family in Terre Haute, Indiana, enchanted audiences at NYC's famed WPA Theatre. Two brothers, Pete and John, live with their parents in a big old house with an attached greenhouse. The father, Dan, has a horticulture business. A pretty young woman named Romy is more or less engaged to marry younger brother Johnny as the play begins, and their prospects look quite rosy, for Johnny has just inherited a ton of money from recently-deceased family friend, Mr. Agajanian. Why, wonders Pete, has Agajanian left his entire estate to Johnny? He starts to persistently ask this question to his mother, Louise. Eventually, Louise does admit that, in fact, Mr. Agajanian was Johnny's father. This news stuns Johnny; but he's not *really* staggered until he goes down to the greenhouse and finds Pete and Romy making love. Pete, it seems, has always desperately wanted Romy; but when she chose Johnny instead he married a woman in the circus who turned out to be a con artist, taking him for everything he had and then disappearing. It seems everyone but Johnny is haunted by a traumatic past experience: Louise by her affair with Agajanian; Dan by the memory of his first true love, a Terre Haute whore; Pete by his failed marriage, and Romy by her *two* failed marriages. (One husband she left; the other was run over by a truckload of chickens [He loved cartoons so much, says Romy, that it was only fitting he should die like Wile E. Coyote.]). And, each character but Johnny knows what he wants. Louise and Dan want the contentment of their marriage; Romy wants to bake bread in a big old house—and she wants Pete, who finally admits that he wants her, too. And, finally, Johnny realizes what he wants. He does not want the money, or Agajanian's house. He wants to go to Nashville to make his own way as a singer of sad—yes, grotesque—love songs in the night. NOTE: this play is a treasure-trove of scene and monologue material.)   (#9925)

CEMENTVILLE
by Jane Martin
Comedy
Little Theatre

(5m., 9f.) Int. The comic sensation of the 1991 Humana Festival at the famed Actors Theatre of Louisville, this wildly funny new play by the mysterious author of *Talking With* and *Vital Signs* is a brilliant portrayal of America's fascination with fantasy entertainment, "the growth industry of the 90's." We are in a run-down locker room in a seedy sports arena in the Armpit of the Universe, "Cementville, Tennessee," with the scurviest bunch of professional wrasslers you ever saw. This is decidedly a small-time operation—not the big time you see on TV. The promoter, Bigman, also appears in the show. He and his brother Eddie are the only men, though; for the main attraction(s) are the "ladies." There's Tiger, who comes with a big drinking problem and a small dog; Dani, who comes with a large chip on her shoulder against Bigman, who owes all the girls several weeks' pay; Lessa, an ex-Olympic shotputter with delusions that she is actually employed presently in athletics; and Netty, an overweight older woman who appears in the ring dressed in baggy pajamas, with her hair in curlers, as the character "Pajama Mama." There is the eager-beaver go-fer Nola, a teenager who dreams of someday entering the glamorous world of pro wrestling herself. And then, there are the Knockout Sisters, refugees from the Big Time but banned from it for heavy-duty abuse of pharmaceuticals as well as having gotten arrested *in flagrante delicto* with the Mayor of Los Angeles. They have just gotten out of the slammer; but their indefatigable manager, Mother Crocker ("Of the Auto-Repair Crockers") hopes to get them reinstated, if she can keep them off the white powder. Bigman has hired the Knockout Sisters as tonight's main attraction, and the fur really flies along with the sparks when the other women find out about the Knockout Sisters. Bigman has really got his hands full tonight. He's gotta get the girls to tear each other up in the ring, not the locker room; he's gotta deal with tough-as-nails Mother Crocker; he's gotta keep an arena full of tanked-up rubes from tearing up the joint—and he's gotta solve the mystery of who bit off his brother Eddie's dick last night. (#5580)

I STAND BEFORE YOU NAKED
by Joyce Carol Oates
Monologues

(Little Theatre) 11f. (doubling possible—original production was done with 6f.) Bare stage. This extraordinary new collection of dramatic monologues by one of America's foremost novelists, poets, essayists and women of letters rivals *Talking With* in dramatic intensity, language and sheer weirdness. The evening begins and ends with the title poem, a haunting evocation of Woman on the edge of the madness of vulnerability. There is humor here, but mostly the monologues grip us in the firm hold of a master writer interested more in the pathetic, the strange, the horrifying. In other words, this is vintage Joyce Carol Oates. Contains the following monologues: "Little Blood Button," "Wife of," "Wealthy Lady," "The Boy," "The Orange," "Good Morning, Good Afternoon," "Darling, I'm Telling You (Angel Eyes)," "Nuclear Holocaust," "Slow Motion," "Pregnant." **(#11681)**

VITAL SIGNS
by Jane Martin
Monologue play

(Little Theatre) 2m., (optional), 6f. Bare stage. The mysterious, pseudonymous Louisvillian, author of the acclaimed *Talking With,* has never been funnier, or more dramatically compelling, than in this extraordinary suite of theatrical miniatures, over thirty monologues with a length of around two minutes each, for six actresses. The two men in the play are "foils" for these compelling women. Although they do speak in one piece, their presence in your cast may be optional. Somehow, all the pieces add up to a collage of contemporary woman in all her warmth and majesty, her fear and frustration, her joy and her sadness. *Vital Signs* wowed them at the Humana Festival at Actors Theatre of Louisville, where its exciting first production was staged by Artistic Director Jon Jory. Included in our book are the details of Mr. Jory's direction which kept the theatrical ball rolling, headed into the pocket for a strike. "It does not just celebrate language from colorful women; [it] does the hoe-down."—Detroit Free Press. The New York Times praised "the continuing vitality and originality of the author's voice." "Offers wonderful opportunities for actresses to show off their versatility."—Washington Times. "Martin's eye and ear for the texture of everyday life in this culture is as playfully accurate as Lily Tomlin and Jane Wagner's. She's a fine quipster; but she manages, too, to open little windows of sadness into women's souls."—Detroit News. **(#24019)**